24 HOURS
THATS ALL IT TAKES

TOSHAN TAMHANE   DR. AJAY TAMHANE

BLUEROSE PUBLISHERS
India | U.K.

Copyright © Toshan Tamhane and Dr. Ajay Tamhane 2024

All rights reserved by author. No part of this publication may be reproduced, stored in a retrieval system or transmitted in any form or by any means, electronic, mechanical, photocopying, recording or otherwise, without the prior permission of the author. Although every precaution has been taken to verify the accuracy of the information contained herein, the publisher assumes no responsibility for any errors or omissions. No liability is assumed for damages that may result from the use of information contained within.

BlueRose Publishers takes no responsibility for any damages, losses, or liabilities that may arise from the use or misuse of the information, products, or services provided in this publication.

For permissions requests or inquiries regarding this publication, please contact:

BLUEROSE PUBLISHERS
www.BlueRoseONE.com
info@bluerosepublishers.com
+91 8882 898 898
+4407342408967

ISBN: 978-93-6261-325-7

Cover Design: Sadhna Kumari
Typesetting: Pooja Sharma

First Edition: August 2024

Preface

When George Mallory, the intrepid mountaineer and probably the first to have reached the top of Mount Everest before Edmund Hillary, was asked why he did something as dangerous as climbing the world's most inhospitable peaks, his answer was simple.

"Because they are there."

That's the simplicity behind the answer to why I wrote this book. An acquaintance of mine dared me to write a book, with the condition that I write it within 24 hours. Nobody had ever asked me to try such a thing. I was tempted but also, I must say, a little daunted.

So, I did what anyone else would do: I googled whether it could be done.

To my surprise, I found numerous guides online on the topic of *How to Write a Book in 24 Hours.*

I was pleased. So, I thought to myself, it could be done.

That's when I decided to do what NIKE tells you to do: ***Just do it***.

Before you get too impressed, let me tell you, dear reader, that there are a couple of caveats to this 24-hour timeline:

1. 24 hours is not a single continuous length of time. I did *NOT* sit down, uninterrupted, over the course of an entire day to write this book. Instead, I wrote it over the course of 21 days – three weeks, to be precise. However, I always timed myself to ensure

that I would complete it within the overall deadline of 24 hours.

2. 24 hours excludes the time taken for the following activities:

   a. Proofreading & substantive editing.

   b. Professional illustrations by the graphic designer.

   c. The general publication processes.

Essentially, 24 hours is the time that it took me to conceptualize, ideate and create the first draft of the entire book, *plus* all sketches of the illustrations and the diagrams. Given this challenge, then, the next thing to ponder was the subject of the book. There were many questions in my mind as I thought about it. *Should it be a book of short stories? A novella? Non-fiction?*

I didn't find any of these ideas appealing.

Finally, I decided to write the kind of book that others might find helpful as a guide or a template for their lives, like a self-help book that you might pick up to help yourself reach a goal. This was more like what I used to do. I've often set and achieved goals for myself, whether it's in the areas of academics, fitness, corporate success, family life or spiritual evolution. I've read extensively about achieving goals and thought it might be best for me to share my thoughts on the best methods to attain a set target.

Naturally, this would be a book that is written in simple, easy language, preferably the kind that you can read within 24 hours!

Think of it this way – who really has the patience to read and understand anything that takes longer than that? That's why we have such a slew of book summaries, video shorts and ten-minute podcasts, right? Hence, I named the book '*24 hours – that's all it takes*'.

Next, I needed a partner. There was no way I could do this on my own. Even Edmund Hillary needed a Sherpa Tenzing Norgay with him when he summitted Everest! So, I asked my father, Dr. Ajay Tamhane, to chip in and become my Sherpa. He has vast expertise on this subject, given his background as a psychologist and his coaching practice, which involves helping diverse individuals, ranging from sportsmen to corporate CXOs and students to meet their professional and personal aspirations. Closer home, he has helped me to achieve several of my own goals. I'm so grateful to him for being a wonderful father. In the journey of writing the book too, he has been absolutely amazing: a contributor, guide, co-author, and constructive critic, all rolled in one.

Thank you, Baba, for this book and everything else that you have done for me. From here on, whenever the pronoun 'I' is used, it means 'We' to signify both of us.

P.S. – This is not to take away from the other two people who have been fundamental to my life's journey. My mother, Jayashree Tamhane and my wife, Deepti. Just enumerating their sacrifices and support could fill an entire book on gratitude!

P.P.S. – Growing up, my father used to often tell me the story of Shantanu and his daughter, Akila. One day, Shantanu returned home, worn out after a strenuous day of work.

Akila, his little sprightly daughter who was 9 years old, saw his exhaustion and quickly got up to make him a cup of coffee. She knew that it was her dad's favourite drink for energy, especially after a hard day of work.

She effortlessly put the filter coffee decoction, a cup of hot milk, a bowl of sugar, and an empty cup with a spoon in a tray. Shantanu watched her curiously. Akila knew exactly how to pour the milk into the cup, then the coffee decoction and a spoonful of sugar, exactly as her father liked it. Then, she added another spoon of sugar – and another – followed by yet another.

"What are you doing, dear?" Shantanu asked in concern, "The coffee will become too sweet!"

Akila replied, "No, Daddy, the coffee will not become sweet. Not yet, at least".

Surprised, Shantanu asked, "Why? You have put at least four cups of sugar into the cup. Why won't it become too sweet, my dear?"

Smiling, Akila replied, "Daddy, until I stir the coffee, it will not become sweet. Most of the sugar will stay at the bottom!".

Just as the coffee will not become sweet unless the sugar is stirred, this book won't be of any help unless you put IT into action. My 24 hours of materials will just stay there, unstirred, unabsorbed, soon forgotten and wasted.

Core Framework:

What would you say to someone who has won a race, competing against 400 million other equally strong participants? If you converted this into a mathematical probability, it implies a 0.00000025% chance! In contrast, your chances of getting into Harvard would have a probability of 3.2%; winning Wimbledon would have a probability of 0.00029% and becoming a dollar millionaire by the age of 50 would have a probability of 4.7%. So, if a person won against 400 million equally able participants, what a victory it is and what a race it would have been, right? Imagine how that person would have felt at the end of such a spectacular achievement? They've beaten everyone else just by surviving. What's more, they've succeeded enough to enjoy the benefits of that struggle.

Now, think of it this way. This is the same race *you* have won too! As humans, each one of us has run this race. It all began when we were first conceived in our mother's wombs. To put it bluntly, when that single sperm emerged victorious to fertilize the ovum, it won against 399,999,999 other competitors. If any other sperm would have won, you would not have been here – nay, you would not be you, but someone totally different. But *you* won right from when you were a zygote. Your reward: life on this earth. You have benefited from the riches, vagaries, and experiences of this planet at the expense of all other equally capable competitors.

What is my point exactly?

It's simple. You are born a WINNER. I am born a WINNER. All of us are BORN WINNERS!

Let me put it another way: each and every one of us was born ONLY because we were WINNERS.

Hence, I firmly believe that continuing to win is our birthright. Yet, unfortunately, many of us forget this. We get lost in the humdrum and mundane struggles of existence, thereby losing out on the biological core of the phenomenal victory that got us on planet Earth in the first place.

That is the main point of this book, and that is what I want to focus on: regaining what is ours, reorienting our sense of achievement and honing our natural winner's mindset.

Over the years, like many of you, I have developed my own mental model for goal setting and winning as follows:

Core Framework for Goal Setting

I. Part A: Prior To Choosing The Goal
    a. Find your motivation – the WHY

    b. Is it the RIGHT WALL to climb?

c. Aim – Knowing EXACTLY what you want

   d. Positive Thinking – BELIEVE in what you set out to do

   e. Negative Thinking – Know what could go WRONG

II. Part B: On The Path Of Achieving The Goal

   a. Visualization – Can you SEE it?

   b. Optimized Training – Do you have the right TOOLS and PLAN?

   c. Ecosystem – Power of the TEAM

   d. Restraint – What will you SACRIFICE for what you want the MOST?

   e. Fear – FACE it

   f. Roll with the PUNCHES

   g. Time Management – power of 60 SECONDS

   h. Energy Management

      1. Sleep

      2. Exercise

      3. Nutrition

      4. Brain Fitness

      5. Meditation

   i. Stress Management

III. Part C: Post Accomplishment Of The Goal

a. Enjoyment of the PROCESS

b. LOSE but don't lose the LESSON

c. Happiness – the FINAL FRONTIER?

Now, the interesting point is that this framework is NOT necessarily sequential – once you achieve the goal, there will always be another one to look forward to. When Edmund Hillary was asked what was the first thought on his mind as he stepped foot on the top of Mount Everest, he said, "All around me I saw so many unclimbed mountains. I immediately started making plans of climbing some of them, including taking paths not traversed so far". This is the power of goals – not achievement but pushing you onwards to set even bigger, better ones!

Throughout the rest of the book, I will go deeper into each facet, explaining the core concept behind it and providing a few effective hacks, quotes & stories to aid the reader. Happy reading 😊

Contents

PART A: PRIOR TO CHOOSING YOUR GOAL 1

1. Motivation 2
2. Right Wall to Climb 10
3. Aim 14
4. Positive Thinking 21
5. Negative Thinking 28

PART B: ON THE PATH OF GOAL ACHIEVEMENT 33

6. Visualization 34
7. Optimized Training: Quantity + Quality + Consistency 40
8. Build an Ecosystem – *The Power of the Team* 46
9. Restraint 54
10. Fear 59
11. Roll with the Punches – Adapt & Evolve, Evolve & Adapt 64
12. Time Management 69
13. Energy Management 77
14. Stress Management 100

PART C: POST GOAL ACHIEVEMENT/ (INITIAL) FAILURE 105

15. Enjoyment of the Process 106

16. Lose – But Don't Lose the Lesson & Never Give Up! 112

17. Happiness – The Final Frontier 117

Acknowledgements (and some Apologies) 127

PART A:
PRIOR TO CHOOSING YOUR GOAL

1. Motivation

Once, a youth asked Socrates, "How will I be sufficiently motivated to achieve my dream of becoming a Greek general?"

Socrates took one look at the youth and asked, "You really want to be a Greek general?"

The youth responded, "Yes, sir. More than anything else in the world."

Beckoning the young man to follow him, Socrates led him to the river. He turned and asked, "I ask you again, are you sure you want to be a Greek general?"

"Yes," the young man replied eagerly, "I definitely want to be a Greek general."

No sooner had the words left his lips than Socrates seized him by the head and shoved him into the river, holding him firmly underwater as he began to struggle madly. Even as water splashed everywhere and the young man's arms flailed wildly, Socrates continued holding him underwater.

Then, he pulled the younger man's wet head up sharply and asked him again, "Do you still want to be a general?"

The young man was coughing violently, gasping for breath, but he repeated, "Yes. Yes, of course, I do!"

Again, Socrates shoved him underwater.

This time, he held him there for a little longer before pulling him up and repeating his earlier question. The young man began to stutter his assent, but Socrates didn't wait for him to finish his sentence. The next time Socrates hauled the young man out for air, he was barely conscious, struggling to breathe. He couldn't form the words to reply to Socrates' sharp questions, muttering, "Air. Air. I need air," before collapsing to the ground. Patiently, the older man waited for him to recover his composure and consciousness. When he did, the young man sprang to his feet, his eyes blazing with rage and confusion.

Socrates merely smiled at him, a twinkle in his eyes. "I am sorry to have put you through this ordeal." He said pleasantly, "But if you really want to be a Greek general, you have to be as desperate for it as you were desperate for air, the third time I held you underwater. When you want something that badly, then nothing else matters. Only then will you get what you truly want – and that, if at all, is how you will become a Greek general."

***

A] Core idea: Unless you want something desperately, you will not do your best for it. The *WHY* behind your dreams is the most critical part of your vision, far more than the *WHAT* and the *HOW*. If you have a goal that challenges you enough, there will inevitably be a point where you are exhausted enough to consider giving up. It is at those moments that you will find the *WHY* of your dreams – why you are on this journey in the first place – driving you onwards.

A few years ago, I decided to run a half-marathon. This was at a time when I had not even run as much as five kilometres! Still, I signed up for an online training program and began following it. The first few days were easy enough. As I checked the schedule, I felt very happy and motivated. It was only after the first ten days that I hit my first bump – an early morning flight and a late-night return flight. In my tiredness, I rationalized that I could hardly run the seven kilometres that I was scheduled to run the next day.

No harm done, right?

Two days later, I had an important meeting, which lasted well beyond midnight. Exhausted, I wasn't able to get up at 6 AM for my strength training session. On the weekend, my mother was unwell, and I had to attend to her. As you can imagine, my weekend's training schedule went out of the window. By the end of the month, with life's distractions and requirements adding up, I had missed a total of six training days. Each of those days had been missed with a perfectly valid excuse. After one more month that passed exactly like this, I gave up entirely. The goal wasn't *that* important, I told myself. In any case, I was more focused on 'overall fitness,' as opposed to running one specific half-marathon. When I put it like this to myself, it made total sense. Actually, it was total bullshit rationalization!

In hindsight, when I thought about it, I wondered what my real motivation had been in choosing that particular goal. Had it been the FOMO of saying, "Yes, I'm also running the 21 kms at the Tata Marathon"? Could it have been the fact that I was the only one among all my friends who had not run at least a half-marathon till that point of time? Had I wanted to prove something to them? As much as I probed my thoughts, though, I couldn't find an easy answer or a really compelling *WHY* behind the choice of my goal. Small wonder then that I had taken the easy way out and given up at the merest hint of difficulty.

***

This reminds me of the legend about the great Maratha king, Chhatrapati Shivaji's trusted lieutenant, Tanaji.

It is said that Tanaji was tasked with capturing the impregnable fort of Kondhana from the Mughals. Along with his maternal uncle, Suryaji, Tanaji led a small group of elite Maratha warriors to scale the fort and fight the Mughals.

During a fierce battle with Uday Bhan, the Mughal general who was in charge of the fort, Tanaji was fatally wounded. Seeing their leader fall, the rest of his men lost their will to fight and began to flee the battle scene. When the dying lieutenant saw this, he called his uncle, Suryaji and managed to whisper something to him before he breathed his last.

Grief-stricken at the death of his nephew, Suryaji now changed the course of the battle, and some historians say, the history of Maratha rule. He cut off the ropes that the Maratha armies had used to climb the fort walls. His men now had no way out.

Turning to the shocked soldiers, Suryaji shouted, "Our brave leader, Tanaji, is no more. You can either join him in death by jumping over the walls, or you can help me fight the Mughals and win the war. Make Tanaji immortal in the annals of history. The choice is yours: a meaningless death or triumph that will be remembered for ages to come."

Inspired, the Marathas put their energies into one heroic last stand, fighting for their lives and pride. Against this force of will, the Mughals were simply doing their duty in defending the fort. Now you tell me, reader, whose motivation was stronger? Who do you think won the war and carried the day? Yes.

The Marathas won the day, founding an empire that would rule large parts of India for the next century and a half.

What is the motto behind a story like this?

When the chips are down, there will be a thousand reasons for you to give up and possibly only ONE for you to continue – that's your WHY. If the WHY is strong, then the WHATs and HOWs will automatically appear and show the way.

Without the WHY, everything is lost.

***

B] Points to note:

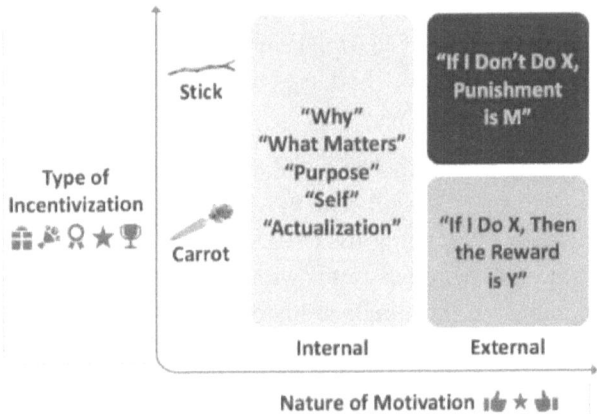

1. There are two types of motivation – internal motivation and external motivation as shown on the X-axis above. Internal motivation is driven by factors that are deeply personal (e.g., desire to prove oneself, life's purpose, a higher sense of drive and mission) whereas external motivation is driven by what others/world wants (e.g., someone you know at work was promoted over you. Now you're motivated to do the same). Of these two, internal motivation is by far more sustainable, but more challenging to generate and maintain. If all motivation is external, then it is also fickle and ever-changing. Your internal drive is the only reliable one in the long run.

2. Motivation is also driven by two types of incentivization forces as shown by the Y-axis of the framework:

    - Carrot forces (or positive incentives) – this refers to the positive benefits of achieving the goal. For example, if you study and come first in the examination, it opens lots of career opportunities for you, not to mention the recognition/fame that this brings.

    - Stick forces (or penalties) – this refers to the negative consequences of NOT achieving the goal. For example, if you don't study and fail, you will lose face among your family and friends, and your job prospects will diminish.

3. Peak performance, then, is the optimal performance that your current ability and expertise can generate in the context of the motivation level that you have. Any further improvement requires either increased

ability (e.g., training more) or superior expertise (e.g., learning a new skill that will help you perform better). The Peak Performance (PP) formula states that

PP = M (A+K),

where PP = Peak Performance; M = Motivation; A = Ability and K = Knowledge.

Hence, mathematically, if M = zero, then no amount of ability and expertise can lead to outstanding performance. When one is at peak performance, it seems as if the output is 'flowing'. As per Mihaly Csikszentmihalyi (the psychologist who coined the term 'flow'), when one is in the flow, one is so involved in the activity that nothing seems to matter, and one can continue to do the activity forever without any reward. Ironically, this is also when the best output is achieved.

C] Quick Hacks:

o **The WHY Charter:** Before you finalize any goal, write down a maximum of 250 words on

- **Why** does the specific goal mean so much to you?
- **What** will happen if you achieve it?
- **What** will happen if you **don't** achieve it?

The answers to these questions will lay the foundation of your will to achieve the goal you have set for yourself. It will also ensure that you stay on the right path despite any failures. Post that charter somewhere you can see daily. Better yet, carry it in your wallet!

- **Motivation Visualization:** Every morning for 10 minutes after you wake up, but *before* you get out of bed:-

    - For the first five minutes, visualize your goal and remind yourself of the **WHY** charter you drew up for yourself.

    - For the next five minutes, visualize the fact that you have achieved that goal. Feel the happiness and joy around that sense of achievement. This can also be done before going to bed or at the end of the day. Personally, I find morning visualization more effective since it helps me anchor myself in the knowledge of what really matters to me. It also helps me anchor the day to what really matters to me before being caught up in the mundane activities of the day.

2. Right Wall to Climb

Anyone can climb a ladder put on a wall. However, putting the ladder on the right wall is an art that cannot be taught, it has to be thought.

A] Core Idea: You may have a goal, an ambition, or a dream. Whatever you might choose to call it, how do you *know* it is the right one? I am not trying to belittle your aspirations, but it is a fact that there are certain 'infeasible walls.' For instance, you might never have trained as an athlete. Then suddenly, at the age of forty, you dream of winning an Olympic medal. Automatically, this dream is *infeasible by context.*

Another example: Let's say you are not a trained musician. You're just an amateur player but dream of playing at the Royal Albert Hall, London in six months. Or, more practically speaking, let's say that you're a junior employee with less than five years of experience working in a multinational company. But you dream of being the CEO of that company within a decade. Both examples are *infeasible by time.*

Then, there are cases that are *infeasible by nature.* Say, for instance, that your mathematical abilities are rudimentary. You have no desire to better those skills, but you also want to score fully in the GMAT exam.

B] Points to Note:

1. It is super-critical to test if your goals are 'right, meaningful and appropriate' (*I am not talking of NOT*

taking a stretch target – we will discuss that in a subsequent chapter)

2. Assume you have two walls (as a metaphor for a goal). You have to choose which wall to climb. If you select wall A, it is important to assess early (preferably before you put a ladder against it!) whether that is the right wall to climb. Later, if you realize that instead of wall A, you had to climb wall B, then it will take you much longer to climb back down, shift your ladder to the other wall and start climbing again from scratch.

3. Put simply, you will save yourself misery, time and resources if you test the wall first and place your ladder accordingly. *Be wise early on or you will be considered otherwise later on.*

The metaphor of the ladder here stands for the efforts that you take for the desired direction toward your goals. If you're in a hurry, you will put the ladder against the wrong wall and end up going in the wrong direction. Therefore, you need to spend enough time deciding which wall is the right one for you.

C] Quick Hacks:

o **Pre-Mortem Analysis:** Every day for at least a week BEFORE you "finalize" your goal, imagine for 15 minutes how it would feel to have actually achieved it. See yourself as having completed your aspiration – what does it feel like? Are you happy? How does your day look? Are you in the 'flow'? What are your biggest worries now?

o **Socratic Testing:** Ask three of your closest friends/ mentors or trusted critics about their views on your potential goal. Are they unanimously supportive? What are their objections? What are their concerns? What advice would they have for you about the journey that you have chosen to undertake? Based on their inputs, you can decide the direction of your goal. This is not to say that *everyone* has to be unanimously supportive; more often than not, there won't be a complete alignment of views. Still, their advice/suggestions will help you modify the wall suitably.

***

On a lighter note…

Once, Mullah Naseeruddin was searching for something under a lit lamp on an otherwise dark street. Soon, a curious crowd gathered.

"Dear Mullah, what are you searching for? We will also help you find what you have lost."

The Mullah smiled and said, "Why, thanks, my friends. So nice of you. I have lost my gold watch, which is very valuable. It would be a disaster if I was unable to find it."

The crowd began to search for his watch, but after an hour of frantic searching, someone asked the Mullah, "But sir, where did you lose your watch? Was it here?

Mullah shook his head slowly. "No, no," He said, "Not at all. In fact, I lost my watch near that ditch." He pointed down the road to a dimly lit area. The crowd was understandably annoyed. "But then, why are you searching for it here?" They demanded irritably.

"Oh, because it was so dark there that I felt it would be easier if we searched under the light!" The Mullah replied calmly.

***

Once, a simple plumber was visiting the Niagara Falls in Canada for the first time. The tour guide explained, in great detail, the miracle of the falls – its height, water flow and impact on surrounding areas. "Various dams, hydroelectric projects and transportation systems surrounding the Niagara Falls constitute one of the largest natural-cum-manmade miracles in the world!"

Listening to this, the plumber sighed and responded, "Such a colossal waste of water. If only someone had thought to plug the leak, it would have been so much better!"

***

3. Aim

The Parrot's Eye
Nothing else matters in comparison with the goal

In the Indian epic, the *Mahabharata*, there is a famous story of Arjuna, the unparalleled archer prince (see above photograph). In this story, the princes were once taken to an archery contest by their guru, Dronacharya. Their task was to hit the wooden parrot in the trees some hundred yards away. Dronacharya called his eager students forward to shoot the target one by one.

The first prince, Yudhishthira, came forward and took aim. However, before he could shoot the arrow, his teacher stopped him and asked, "Wait. First, tell me, what can you see ahead of you?"

To this, the prince replied, "Revered teacher, I can see the trees, the blue sky, the plain ground and all the birds ahead of me." Shaking his head, Dronacharya replied,

"Put your bow and arrow down. Go back and stand in the line."

The second prince, Duryodhana, came forward, and he, too, took aim. Again, he was stopped by Dronacharya, who asked the same question he had asked to Yudhishthira.

"Teacher, I see everything with my eyes," Duryodhana responded, "I see you, I see my brothers, and I see the blue skies. I see the river, and, in the distance, I see the mountains."

Dronacharya told Duryodhana to put down his bow and arrow and step back. Duryodhana protested, but he was told that it was pointless to argue.

This same routine continued for a while. Each of the princes stepped forward, took aim, answered wrongly and were told to step back. By now, everyone was thoroughly confused. They had been told this was an archery contest. They had prepared accordingly, and now, none of them were being allowed to shoot. This was truly strange!

Finally, it was Arjuna's turn. Dronacharya asked him the same question. Arjuna responded, "Teacher, I see nothing but the eye of the parrot that my arrow is going to hit."

"Don't you see me, your teacher? Don't you see your beloved brothers? How can you be so blind, Arjuna?" Dronacharya asked, clearly goading Arjuna.

The young prince was unfazed.

"No," he said calmly, "I see nothing but the eye of the parrot."

Dronacharya smiled, "Then shoot, dear Arjuna, the best of archers!"

Arjuna shot his arrow, unerringly hitting the eye of the parrot in its centre.

"Bravo, bravo, Arjuna!" Dronacharya applauded him. Turning to his other students, he asked, "Princes, do you see what has just happened? All of you tried to shoot, but your eyes and soul were not focused on the only thing that mattered: your goal or your aim. Nothing else should be visible to you as archers except that goal and aim. Even if you had released your arrows, you would never have been able to hit the target. You were not focused like Arjuna. That is why he will become the greatest of all archers that ever walked this land."

***

A] **Core Idea**: If you don't know where you want to go, how will you ever get there? Life and its milestones can definitely be lived through serendipity and happenstance, but given that you live only once, do you want to take such a chance? That is why it is so important to have a crystal-clear aim.

B] **Points to Note:**

1. The purpose of your aim should be two-fold. Firstly, you should know exactly what you want to achieve, and secondly, everyone around you who is a stakeholder should also be clear about your aims. Simply put, there must be complete alignment between you and your stakeholders on the targets that you are focusing on. Otherwise, it will be a replay of that old story about five blind men and an elephant. This will become even more important if the goal is a *team* goal as opposed to an individual goal.

2. Doing something without an aim is NOT BAD. It is just that it will not be as effective, especially if you want that action to lead to continuous improvements and tangible benefits. Say you run daily for five or ten kilometres, but you never see any health benefits beyond a certain 'maintenance' point. You haven't set an aim for yourself, so you are just running to keep yourself healthy. On the other hand, if you do set an aim, then running will become a potent tool for helping to make you into a better version of yourself.

3. With a clear aim in mind, you have more reasons NOT to skip that 5 or 10 km run when you are feeling slightly off or if you are travelling. That aim keeps reminding you that you HAVE to do it. It is not optional.

C] Quick Hacks:

- **SMART Aims**

    - <u>S – Specific</u>. This is not vague or general. For example, rather than saying, "I want to improve my public speaking," you say, "I want to speak effectively in front of the entire top management at the Annual Day function three months from today."

    - <u>M – Measurable</u>. This means that you can measure your goal with clear improvement metrics. So, instead of saying, "I want to lose weight," you say, "I want to reduce to 85 kgs from 102 kgs in 6 months." The more specific your aim is, the easier it is to set measurable targets (including interim ones)

- A – Ambitious. Don't negotiate against yourself – be bold in your aspiration-setting. This is called Big Hairy Audacious Goals – when someone hears it, they should go, "Wow – that's something. Are you sure you want to do this?" When Bill Gates said, "The goal of Microsoft is to put a computer in every home and on every desk," everyone ridiculed him. But for those who worked with him, it was both a rallying call and a mission. That was more than three decades ago, and since then, Microsoft has definitely achieved what Gates wanted in more ways than one. Wouldn't you agree?

- R – Realistic. This is the counterbalance to Ambitious. You can't aim to run 100 meters in ten seconds unless you are Usain Bolt! So, your goal has to be big enough to make jaws drop but realistic enough for you (and others) to take it seriously. Going back to my example about reducing weight, a goal like "I want to reduce to 85 kgs from 102 kgs in 6 months from today" meets a realistic criterion. On the other hand, if you say you want to achieve the same goal in, say, *three* days, then obviously, that will be unrealistic. After all, even the natural laws of science have their limitations!

- T – Timebound. Unless there is a restriction of time, motivation and urgency do not exist. No one is moved by a goal that can be achieved 15 years from now. This is not to say that you cannot have an uber goal, say, of winning the Nobel Prize in Literature in ten years. But you will have to break that down into interim, time-aligned steps of writing your first book in a year.

- **Public Statement of the Aim**: While not being overtly focused on the dissemination or the public relations aspect, the objective of this hack is to use public 'naming and shaming' as a way to prevent you from reneging on your promises to yourself. The fact that people will ask you about it everywhere you go is a good deterrent for you NOT to backtrack. The more public your statement is, the more difficult it will be for you to give excuses later.

- **Visible Monitoring Tools**: These could be physical charts or diaries that measure progress or group apps (e.g., Strava) where others can also view your efforts. Today, there are thousands of tracking tools, depending on the activities you undertake. On the professional front, you have project management tools and Red-Amber-Green Trackers, which achieve the same purpose. If it is visible, it will get done. This is more difficult if your goal is slightly more internal (e.g., improving your relationship with your boss). However, in that case, monitoring your progress will be a little difficult, and that is, after all, the crux of this hack.

> *"Not failure, but low aim, is a crime."* (James Russell Lowell)
>
> *"Aim for the moon. If you miss, you may hit a star".* (W. Clement Stone)
>
> *"Aim high – the future you see, is the person you will be."* (Jim Cathcart)
>
> *"Do not aim at small goals to achieve greatness, that's not possible. The tougher the goal, the stronger the seeker."* (Anonymous)
>
> *"Setting goals is the first step in turning the invisible into the visible."* (Tony Robbins)

4. Positive Thinking

Two frogs, Tom and Tim, were basking in the summer sun near a pond. Tom was young and optimistic, while Tim was older and more pessimistic. As Tom was hopping around the pond, he fell into a bucket that someone had left out. He tried to jump out, but the bucket was too deep. When Tim hopped over, he saw Tom struggling.

"It's useless," said Tim, "You'll never get out of there."

"Don't be silly," said Tom. "Someone will surely come and get me out."

Just then, a little boy walked by and heard Tom's calls for help. He lifted the bucket and tipped it over, freeing the frog. Tom hopped happily away, calling out to Tim, "I told you I'd get out! A positive outlook always pays off."

***

A] Core Idea: Unless you can think optimistically about meeting your goals, there will be no chance that you will be able to achieve them. That's why, after AIM, the most important thing is to think positively – that you *can* achieve whatever target you set.

Power Of Belief

In your mind, you must *see* yourself doing it. Everything in this world is created twice: first, in the mind of the creator, and second, in reality. What others will see is the second creation, not the first one. If you cannot even see the success of your aim in your own mind, there is no chance that you will ever see it in reality. More often than not, we are not even able to see that possibility in our mind's eye.

From a metaphysical standpoint, every thought creates a 'split' in the multi-verse – so if you see and believe that you can achieve something, then somewhere, in some version of reality, you are already achieving that goal. This will enhance your chances of doing the same in this 'original verse,' so the theory goes.

But why is positive thinking so difficult? Well, that's because we are often caught amidst a flurry of negative thoughts, emotions, and influences. Being able to extract oneself from the quicksand of daily negativity and imagine a future of possibilities is half the battle won. This is not to say that positivity alone is enough to attain success. Despite all the positivity in the world, things may still not go our way. My main point is that without positivity and at least a bit of optimism, there is no real chance that *anything* will go your way.

Thus, positivity is a *necessary*, if not *sufficient*, solution.

B] Points to Note:

1. The mind is a very powerful and strange phenomenon. Whatever is happening around you does not affect the mind as much as the other way around: it is the mind that influences your reality. We often hear that phrase, don't we? *So-and-so really bent reality to her will to achieve greatness.* Yes, stalwarts and icons across fields have often been able to unleash the power of their positive thinking to change their circumstances.

2. Positive thinking is NOT mere wishful thinking. It is a deep concentration of thoughts aimed at assuming that the chosen target has already been achieved or is being achieved against all odds.

3. Positive thinking is NOT dreaming. It is consciously choosing to believe and to express the belief that one will succeed tomorrow, no matter how bad today might be.

4. As you think, so you feel, and as you feel, so you behave. So, if we need to change our behaviour, we must start before, in the realm of thought. That's where positive thinking comes in.

***

Once, a massive elephant was straining against the thick rope around its ankle, trying in vain to break free. A young girl noticed the elephant's distress and approached its handler. "Why does this elephant not just use its strength to break the rope and escape?" she asked.

The handler smiled and replied, "When this elephant was just a baby, it was tied with the same rope. At that time, the rope was strong enough to restrain the little elephant. It has grown up firmly believing that that same rope can still hold it, even though now it could easily snap the rope."

The elephant's limited belief in the power of the rope had imprisoned it for life. Like the elephant, many of us go through life trapped by false assumptions and self-imposed limitations. Unless we can think positively to overcome our own 'chains and ropes', we can never achieve our full potential.

***

C] **Quick Hacks:**

- **The *Bhagavad Gita* Hack**: In the Indian epic, *Mahabharata*, Lord Krishna urges Arjuna to fight the vast armies of the Kauravas. However, Arjuna hesitates. He had lost his will to fight and instead makes one excellent excuse after another. To overcome this, Lord Krishna narrates the Bhagavad Gita, a set of verses which help Arjuna rebuild his confidence while at the same time explaining various concepts of duty, victory, etc. One of the main themes of the Gita involves Lord Krishna urging Arjuna to do a kind of post-event visualisation. He tells him that his enemies are already dead and shows him a scenario of life with their evil enemies already vanquished. Krishna explains that all Arjuna now has to do is follow his destiny. This positive visualisation encourages

Arjuna to believe that the task ahead of him is not difficult, but one that *has to happen*, come what may. He is the only means to achieve the Divine Will. This hack is especially powerful if one already has a religious or spiritual bent of mind.

- **1000 repetitions per day chant**: This is often used by sportsmen – they keep repeating the goal again and again to charge themselves up, similar to Muhammad Ali's "I am the best" or "I am the champion of champions" chant which Ali apparently said over 100,000 times every single day. Psychologists have concluded that such a high degree of repetition is effective in convincing the mind-body axis that the statement being repeated is already reality. Take, for instance, the popular legend of one of London's most enterprising mayors, Dick Whittington. Legend has it that this once-poor orphan used to sit at the foot of Highgate Hill, where he heard the pealing of the Bow Bells at London's St. Mary-le-Bow Church. With each peal, he told himself, "Turn again, Whittington, once Lord Mayor of London! Turn again, Whittington, twice Lord Mayor of London! Turn again, Whittington, thrice Lord Mayor of London!". A few decades later, Whittington and the peals of the Bow Bells became a reality when Dick Whittington indeed became the Mayor of London.

***

Two seeds are at the root of this story.

The first seed was a positive thinker. She wanted to get off the ground, to grow and explore life. Whatever happened in life, she was up for everything, confident that the world outside was a better place than the dark underground. She dreamed that a wonderful life existed for her outside the soil. So, she grew. Her life was as she had imagined, colourful and wonderful. She did encounter problems once in a while, but her heart was happy about her choice to get off the ground.

Then there was the other seed. Unlike the first seed's enthusiastic approach to the possibilities ahead, the other seed sat in her shell underground, worrying. She was distressed about the dangers she may encounter if she left the ground, about being exposed to too much sun, or the predators that might harm her outside of her comfort zone. Because her head was full of worries, she didn't go anywhere. She played it safe and waited. Then, one day, a hen wandered near the spot where the second seed sat hidden underground. Discovering the seed, the hen ate it immediately.

Both seeds got exactly what they thought despite their starting circumstances being identical. Only their thoughts and attitude made the difference!

***

> *"Whatever the mind can conceive and believe, it can achieve."*
> *(Norman Vincent Peale)*
>
> *"Don't be pushed around by the fears in your mind. Be led by the dreams in your heart." (Roy T. Bennett)*
>
> *"Impossible is nothing but I'M POSSIBLE." (Anonymous)*
>
> *"Every day comes bearing its own gifts. Untie the ribbons." (Ann Ruth Schabacker)*
>
> *"Only a positive outlook may not change everything – however, it is far superior to the alternative in terms of motivating you to fight on." (Dr. Ajay Tamhane)*

5. Negative Thinking

A] Core Idea: All of us have heard about the power of positive thinking in books, podcasts, speeches, presentations, and in this book, too! There is nothing new about positive thinking. However, its reverse concept – negative thinking – can also be a great weapon in our arsenal if we leverage it suitably. Now, most of us see negative thinking as a *BAD* thing. Possibly, since the word negative is associated with the word 'bad', it is something to be avoided at all costs. For instance, we often try to stop ourselves from a spiral of negative thinking. Thousands of quotes on the Internet will tell us to think positively, but there is nothing that encourages us to think negatively! This has ensured that one of the most powerful concepts is hidden from us. On the other hand, I believe that it is important that we be exposed to negative thinking, albeit with a twist!

Negative thinking opens one of our primal energies: the aversion to DEFEAT, DISAPPOINTMENT, and DEJECTION. These are emotions that we all hate to go through, and as a species, we are programmed to avoid them at all costs. In fact, the pull of negative feelings is more powerful than the push of positive ones. Biologists credit the sympathetic nervous system with the 'fight or flight response', which has ensured human survival in the face of all dangers over the last several thousand years. As soon as humans saw something, say a yellow movement in the bushes, their physiological systems would assume 'the worst' (say, a lion or a cheetah) and take defensive action (get ready to fight or start running). This ensured that we would not get impacted if the yellow movement was a predator – if it was a deer, then we were safe in any case. Heads, I win, Tails, you lose!

From a different disciplinary view, economists recognize the phenomenon of 'loss aversion'. Man hates to lose more than he likes to win. Hence, if one has $100 and loses $50, it will likely feel worse than if one had $0 and gained $50, although the outcome is exactly the same. In life, this 'negative thinking' drives so much behaviour that it is its own motivational force. For example, a person decides not to try a new restaurant because they are afraid of being disappointed, even though they know it could be a great experience. The person is more concerned with avoiding the potential loss of a good dining experience than with the potential gain of trying something new and potentially enjoyable. Similarly, a person decides not to try a new hobby because they fear failing, even though they know it could be fun and rewarding. The person is more concerned with the potential *loss* of self-esteem or embarrassment than with the potential *gain* of learning a new skill or hobby.

The key is to use this power of negative thinking in OUR FAVOUR instead of against us – and it is possible to turn 'NEGATIVE' into a 'POSITIVE.'

B] Points to Note:

1. Negative thinking, if done right, opens us to the possibilities of what may happen IF certain things are not done. If you don't work hard today and develop lazy habits, of course, your life trajectory is going to be a downhill one.

2. Negative thinking keeps us on our guard. This concept is used in various arenas, including:

   a. Pre-mortem analysis (discussed earlier) – visualize the future if you don't achieve success. How do you feel about it? Why did it happen? What can be done to prevent it?

   b. In worst-case scenarios – of course, we should hope for the best BUT we must prepare for the worst. Hope is not a strategy, but preparing for the worst is!

3. We do not always need to dwell on negative thoughts– however, a certain amount of mental energy needs to be spent on thinking of a 'bad future outcome.' If this charges you up, scares you sufficiently and motivates you to get off your ass and do the right things, then the purpose is achieved.

C] Quick Hacks:

o **Broken Glass Meditation**: It is said that the Buddha pioneered this approach. He would often go to the cremation ground and see hundreds of bodies being burnt. He would visualize his own body as being one of them – and in this way, it is said that he overcame his fear of death. Incidentally, in behavioural psychology, the name of this process is desensitization, which uses what modern psychology terms as Cognitive Behaviour Therapy (CBT). To enable his disciples to get similar benefits, the Buddha would ask his disciples to meditate with a broken glass in front, especially since he felt that the crematorium method was too harsh for an ordinary man. The broken glass symbolised life. The Buddha would ask his disciples to visualize a "broken and shattered life," full of sorrows, troubles and torment. He always insisted on feeling the sadness and the grief. Many disciples broke down in tears; some were inconsolable for hours on end. The process was cathartic for many of his disciples. The broken glass method made them mentally stronger and better positioned to face life and its fears if and when they occurred.

- **The Redgrave method:** Sir Steve Redgrave is often regarded as the 'best Olympian ever'. He won gold medals in 5 consecutive Olympic Games starting from 1984 to 2000, a longevity feat never repeated. One of his techniques was to do a negative analysis on "Why will Britain NOT win the gold medal?" He would get his fellow rowers to list the reasons, some of which could be:

  - I will have an upset stomach on the day of the finals.
  - My mother will die the night before.
  - The team will get drunk the night before.
  - One of the team members will sprain his wrist.
  - … and so on. At one time, Redgrave listed over 370 reasons why the team won't win a gold medal. He then went on to write the mitigation factor of each of these reasons, including:
  - Stomach upset on day of finals [No food experimentation – same food for the entire month prepared by the same chef with same ingredients tested at least 1 year in advance]

- My mother will die on the night before [Hold a group therapy session where the player imagines the death of the mother, does a funeral speech and then goes out to row for his mother's spirit. Repeat the process over and over so that the news of death is no longer a shock but a trigger for superior performance]

As Sir Redgrave said, "When all the negative reasons for non-victory are struck off, all that remains is the opposite – VICTORY."

> *"When you suppress negative thoughts, you are also suppressing your ability to deal with the fallout, should they become real." (Dr Ajay Tamhane)*
>
> *"While positive thoughts are better than negative thoughts, one does not go into battle hoping that the enemy will miss all the shots that he takes." (Special forces prep phrase)*
>
> *"Convert negative thinking into a plan of action – only then can you use these thoughts to rise like the Phoenix." (Dr Ajay Tamhane)*
>
> *"Hope for the Best, but prepare for the Worst." (old saying)*

PART B:
ON THE PATH OF GOAL ACHIEVEMENT

6. Visualization

Mullah Naseeruddin was walking through the forest when he came across a giant tree.

Tired, he sat down in its shade, saying, "I wish I could drink some cool water right now."

Lo and behold! A jug of the sweetest, freshest water appeared before him. The Mullah was surprised but delighted. He took a deep drink from the jug, saying, "That takes care of my thirst, but what about food? I wish there were some dosas for me to eat."

No sooner had he said the words than dosas, along with side dishes – chutney and sambar appeared before him. Even more surprised, the Mullah ate the food and burped in satisfaction. "Now that my hunger and thirst have been slaked," he said aloud, "I wish there was a bed on which I could take a nap."

Immediately, a bed furnished with a comfortable mattress and pillows appeared out of nowhere.

The Mullah got into bed, stretched his legs, tucked himself in, ready to take a nap. All of a sudden, he thought, "What if all this vanished and a tiger came to eat me?"

You can imagine what happened next....

Moral: Our minds are exactly like the wishing tree under which the Mullah was able to manifest everything he wished for – whether we wish for drinks, water, and a bed or a hungry tiger, it is up to us! The mind has the power to bring to reality anything that we visualize – what we visualize is up to us!

***

A] **Core Idea:** If you want to achieve something, you have to be able to visualize it happening. As I have said before, everything in the world is created twice – first in the mind of the creator and only then in the real world.

Visualization is not the same as dreaming – visualization is the act of consciously "seeing, feeling and believing" the goal, while dreaming is merely a wish.

B] **Points to Note:**

1. Since time immemorial, scientists, pseudo-scientists and religious/ faith believers have been talking about the power of visualization. From their respective vantage points, these different disciplines have focused on getting us to 'see first, achieve later'.

2. There are several stories of celebrities, like Muhammad Ali, who called himself the 'heavyweight champion of the world' even before he fought his first professional fight. Another example is that of Jim Carrey, who wrote a cheque of USD 1 million to himself when he was still struggling to get roles in C-grade movies. He encashed it more than a decade later but he did encash it for sure!

3. From a purely scientific standpoint, there may be no proof as to why this works today – however, from the point of psychology, there is immense power in visualizing that you have already achieved the goal you have set out to achieve.

***

Once, the King's Minister was passing a stone quarry where huge stones were being broken.

He saw a man labouring hard to break a large rock. He asked the man, "Noble Sir, what are you up to?". The man replied in an irritated voice, "I am breaking a stone into smaller pieces. Isn't that obvious?"

Nodding and thanking the stonebreaker, the Minister moved on. A few minutes later, he saw another man breaking a larger rock. Curious, he went to him and asked the same question. This man turned, smiled and said, "Sir, I am creating the raw material that can be transported to town easily to build the temple."

Thanking the second stonebreaker, the Minister moved on. Ahead, he saw a third man going hard at a gigantic rock, much larger than the ones he had seen before. And yet, there was something different about this man. He was smiling, singing and going about his task in a carefree manner.

He asked the third stonebreaker the same question. The man paused, then bowed before the rock and turned to answer. With a smile on his face and a twinkle in his eye, he said, "I am carving out the image of Lord Krishna from this rock for the town temple. It's almost there – just needs some finishing touches. It will take me a few days – but oh, how lucky am I that I can use my strength to create the image of God!"

The Minister bowed to the as-yet uncut, uncarved image and moved ahead. He had no doubt as to which rock-breaker he wanted to work on the King's palace. The power of the third stone-cutter's visualization had convinced the Minister as to whose craftsmanship would be the best for his purpose.

***

C] Quick Hacks:

o **Make 'News' Of Your Dream:** Take an old edition of a 'relevant magazine' (e.g., *Wall Street Journal*, *Sports Illustrated*) and tear out the cover page. Now, take a photo of yourself, in the outfit that you might be wearing the day you accomplish your goal. Paste your photo on the cover page. Now frame it and place it near your bed. When you go to bed each night, look at that photo. Repeat your goal to yourself fifty times. Repeat the process every morning.

Make Your Dream "Newsworthy"

o **Auto-Suggestion Though Self-Hypnosis:** Hypnosis is another powerful method for visualization. It involves a three-stage process:

1. Fixation: Fix your attention on an ongoing process for example, breathing or music. Concentrate fully on the specific process at hand.

2. Relaxation: Progressively relax each part of your body, from your head to your toes, as you let go of all mental stresses, tensions, and

worries. Your body and mind need to be in a state of ease and comfort.

3. Visualization: See your goal clearly. Give yourself positive affirmations regarding the achievement of your goal. This could be sentences you say to yourself like:

   a. "I am getting better and better every day."

   b. "I am feeling very happy given that I just completed…."

   c. Everyone around me is congratulating me on…."

o **Post Achievement Story**: Write a story of what happened moments AFTER you achieved your goal. Describe vividly how you see the surrounding environment. Use all the 5 sensory inputs:

- See the medal you got

- Hear the claps and the pride in people's voices as they tell you, "Wow, you did it!"

- Taste the champagne you will be drinking, the chocolates and the sweets that you are eating

- Smell the perfume of the people around you as they hover to take selfies

- Tell yourself this every day and each time you finish a task related to your goal

- Feel the victory champagne spilling on your skin – what a thrill!

***

The CEO of a global shoe company once sent a salesman to an African island nation to study the market opportunity. The salesman returned, disappointed, after a few weeks, saying, "There is no opportunity there. Nobody on the island wears shoes."

Not fully convinced, the CEO sent another salesman to the island to validate the first findings. The second salesman returned after just a few days, very elated and said, "There's a great opportunity here! Nobody wears shoes, so we can generate a need for shoes and capture 100% of the market."

Still a bit suspicious, the CEO sent a third salesman. A high-performer and ambitious professional, the third salesman returned after a month and said, "There is a gigantic opportunity here since nobody wears shoes. They don't even use currency of any kind, so we may have a problem with getting paid for our sales. However, they do have lots of leather and jute resources, which we can use to make the shoes. So, we need to put a barter system in place. I'd say there is a realistic opportunity here."

The CEO immediately moved to action!

Three different salesmen had gone to the same island nation, yet it was their individual power to dream and visualise that made all the difference.

***

> *"Whatever the mind can conceive and believe, it can achieve." (Normal Vincent Peale)*
>
> *"Whatever the mind can visualize, it can actualize." (Dr. Ajay Tamhane)*
>
> *"Everything is created twice. First in the mind and then in reality." (Robin Sharma)*

7. Optimized Training: Quantity + Quality + Consistency

A] Core Idea: Being good – or even great at something is not always just a result of innate talent or passion. One has to train like hell for it, regardless of whether it's a skill like coding or playing a sport. You have probably heard of Malcolm Gladwell's 10,000 hours rule: *To be proficient at something, you need to put in at least 10,000 hours of effort into the activity.*

However, it is not just quantity but also the quality of effort that matters. Hard work is necessary but not sufficient. Similarly, your natural smarts can only get you so far if you are not prepared to put in the hours and be "ready for the grind," as they say. Hence, the concept of optimised training. What does this mean, you might ask. It means asking yourself if you are training the right way, with the right guidance, for the right time. Even Eliud Kipchoge cannot keep winning marathons without this combination. He must put in the hours, but he must use those hours for the right things in the right way.

B] Points to Note:

1. Difference between Hard & Smart work:

    i. Hard work indicates the quantum of effort you put into your training – the intensity of activities that one undertakes to fulfil ambition, often referred to as the 'sweat, toil and tears' of the achiever.

ii. Smart work indicates the appropriateness or suitability of the effort. For exaggeration purposes, if you set a goal to become a faster swimmer, then lifting weights in the gym, no matter how hard you go at it, will not help you achieve your goal.

2. Whatever your skill level, it is foolhardy to train without a coach & a training plan. Even the most elite performers in their respective fields have coaches/ guides/ mentors who can do a whole host of things for them:

    i. Push them/goad them.

    ii. Help them find gaps/ areas of improvement.

    iii. Provide an honest critique – especially if you are a top-class performer, who is going to tell you what's wrong?

3. Consistency is the glue that binds quantity and quality. Champions do not train 'when they feel like it'. The real magic happens when one trains even when one does not feel like it, and when no one is watching. That's also the difference between motivation and discipline – in the case of the former, you are excited to do something that needs to be done whereas in the case of the latter, you do it, irrespective of moods, feelings, and desires. Why? Because it is the right thing to do.

C] Quick Hacks:

o **Training Log:** Maintain a log where you honestly capture your daily performance/ routine. This is useful whether you are training for a triathlon or learning a new language. Unless you track your daily progress, the weeks and months will fly by without you realizing it. Kilian Jornet, the world's top ultra-marathoner and speed runner, has training logs dating more than two decades ago when he was still an amateur.

- **Interim Milestones**: Have as many internal milestones as you can. For example, if you are preparing for a marathon in 24 weeks, make sure you have markers for your half marathon, 25K and 35K runs (most beginner marathon programs don't need you to run more than 30-35k in training). Only one final marker of success is too risky a measure without breaking it into interim parts.

- **Learning from Precedents:** Most likely, you will not be the first one to target a specific goal. Hence, you will have (or should search and get) potential role models who have 'been there, done that'.

    - What can you learn from them? What is it that made them successful? Was it some technique or realization that you can benefit from?

    - Are you doing the things they did? How closely are you following their habits, timetables and activities? If you are differing, then why?

- **Jerry Seinfeld's 'Don't break the streak' routine**: Whatever your goal, do something towards it daily. Seinfeld, recognized as one of the best comics in the world, makes it a point to write his jokes and stand-up routine for a small amount of time every single day without fail. No excuses or reasons. It is not the amount of time (i.e., as little as 15 mins) that matters but the consistency behind it. That's the price of being the highest paid comedian in the world – the sheer volume of consistent hard work. As Seinfeld said, "I don't want to be 100% better in a year, just 1% better each day. For this, I have to practice every day."

- **3 Es**:
  - Experience: Be willing to go through the entire motion. Don't question the training plan until you have gone through it entirely, especially if it is designed in conjunction with an expert.

  - Enjoy: Training is tough, and training for superhuman goals is brutal if you do not enjoy the process. You need to like the training – the journey is as important as the end goal, and training is your journey. Often, I am asked how one can like intense efforts. Getting up early & going out for a run while training for a marathon is so tough – one may do it nevertheless, but it is definitely not enjoyable! The only way one can enjoy the training is to keep the end goal in mind. Why are you doing it? If the WHY is important enough, then you can enjoy the toughest of HOWs. Else, it's a massive struggle that causes most folks to give up soon.

  - Explore: Over time, don't hesitate to explore new avenues and activities in the training. This will also reduce the boredom and monotony of your training.

***

Beethoven was once on a vacation after a gruelling concert schedule.

Yet, on day 2, he played the piano for more than 4 hours despite being exhausted and ill. His neighbour was amazed but said nothing.

The next day, Beethoven played the piano for more than 6 hours and remarked, "Thank God, I am on holiday", before he retired for the day. Again, the neighbour heard this and said nothing at all. The next morning, over breakfast, the neighbour could no longer contain his curiosity. He asked, "Ludwig, why do you train so hard every day, especially when you are supposed to relax during your vacation?"

Beethoven smiled and replied, "What would you have me do? Take a break from music?"

The neighbour said, "Sure, at least for a few days. You are the best in the world. Surely you can afford that?"

Beethoven's face changed. He looked grim and responded, "Sadly, it does not work that way. If I take a day off, I notice the difference in my music. If I take a week off, the critics will notice the difference. If I take a month off, the audience will notice the difference. So no, there can't be any off time".

The neighbour didn't know what to say. He got up to pour some tea. As he took the cup, Beethoven added with a wry smile, "This is my vacation – why else would I be playing for only 4-6 hours instead of my normal 10-12 hour routine?".

***

"I worked hard day and night for 4 years just to experience the glory of 9 seconds." (Usain Bolt)

"Don't decrease the goal – increase the effort." (Tom Coleman)

"Suffer now in training and live the rest of your life as a champion." (Muhammad Ali)

"The butterfly is nothing but a caterpillar who went through the concentration camp of Auschwitz". (Anonymous)

"There is no glory in practice, but without practice, there is no glory." (Anthony Joshua)

"I only start counting when it hurts." (Ali – on how many crunches does he do")

"I do not know anyone who has got to the top without hard work. That is the recipe. It will not always get you to the top, but should get you pretty near." (Margaret Thatcher)

I'm a great believer in luck, and I find the harder I work the more I have of it." (Thomas Jefferson)

"If you really look closely, most overnight successes took a long time." (Steve Jobs)

8. Build an Ecosystem – *The Power of the Team*

"TEAM- Together Empowering to Achieve More"

A] **Core idea:** Achieving goals is NOT a solo task – even for the most 'solo' of goals, a TEAM is always required. The better the team around you, the better your chances of success.

For example, if your goal is simple, for instance, cracking a prestigious competitive examination, like that of the Institute of Chartered Accountants of India (the Indian version of the CPA equivalent for the United States), the minimum number of people you need around you is more than five, as follows:

- A teacher/ coach/ guide who can teach you the right subjects and tutor you along the journey.

- 1-2 family members who know the kind of commitment you need to have and who are understanding when you miss key functions or keep crazy schedules.

- 1-2 friends (or co-applicants) who are there to encourage you, share their experiences and give you the sense that 'you are not alone'.

A much-talked-about case study is that of the town of Kota and how it produces IIT-Joint Entrance Examination (JEE) toppers and high-listers year after year. These entrance examinations to the Indian Institutes of Technology, are probably the toughest academic examinations anywhere in the world, and less than 0.02% of applicants make it out of 11,00,000 applying each year. While this seems to be an abysmally low success rate, the percentage of successful applicants from the town of Kota is 1000X superior. Why is this the case? The answer lies in the fact that there is a community geared to enable the applicant to succeed in the JEE examinations. There is the obvious FOMO factor that makes one study hard, given the 10,000+ students who come to Kota to study each year. However, beyond this, it is the question of the right ecosystem that surrounds the aspirant. This covers not only tutors for the various subjects but also the landlords who give out their apartments on rent to aspirants, the restaurants who supply food and stay open late into the night to cater to hungry, tired students and the helpers who wash clothes and perform odd jobs so that there is little time required away from studies. It is as if the entire town wants you to succeed.

Taking another extreme illustration, for a goal like winning an Olympic medal in a solo sport like the 42 km marathon, elite runners will have a core team of ~15+ people, including:

- 2-3 pacers
- 1 manager
- 1 head coach
- 1 physiotherapist (can double up as a massage practitioner, or there could be a separate one)
- 1 nutritionist
- 1 psychologist

- 1 strength & conditioning coach
- 1 cook + 1 helper
- 1 logistics/admin caretaker
- 2-3 family members for support

B] Points to Note:

1. Types of team members – who to have on the team:

   a. Expertise-driven team members: Some of the team/ecosystem members join in due to their expertise and area of specialization. In the marathon example, the physio and the head coach are experts in their respective fields. Their expertise is a result of education & experience.

   b. Comfort-care-friendship driven team members: Some of the members perform subtler psychological roles, viz. listening to frustrations, being there when the athlete is down, and celebrating small triumphs on the road to success. In the earlier case, this would be the role played by the athlete's family members.

2. Ensuring the right mix and complementarity of the ecosystem is the key – the last thing an athlete will want to do is to spend time solving issues and friction between team members. Hence, the team has to be integrated based on (1) and (2), but it is equally important to clarify roles if required. You do not want your father to become your psychologist or your mother to take charge of your diet unless it is their area of expertise.

3. Check for all the expertise areas you need – trainer, coach for specific activities, therapist, etc. Never leave any key area open. It is better to ask an expert for recommendations since they are more likely to recommend experts they like and are comfortable working together.

4. Always ask for references and credentials. Take time in selection – once selected, subsequent replacement is extremely difficult as well as emotionally painful.

5. However, if the team member does not gel well, do not hesitate to replace them. A rotten apple spoils the whole basket in no time! Moreover, it is important to do the replacement as fast as possible – *Fail the Failure Faster*.

6. Have clear & aligned goals for the entire team. Every member needs to know why they are there and what success looks like.

***

Four Seasons & a Croissant

Steve Wynn, the billionaire founder of Wynn Resorts & Casinos, shares a story of his family's vacation in Paris. The Wynn family was staying at the Four Seasons and had ordered breakfast in bed. His daughter only ate half of a croissant, leaving the other half for later. Wynn and his family left to explore Paris, and upon returning to the hotel room, the pastry was gone. His daughter was disappointed, assuming housekeeping had got rid of it.

On the telephone, there was a message from the front desk. They said that housekeeping had removed the half-eaten croissant from the room, assuming that upon arrival, they would prefer a fresh pastry. So, the front desk contacted the kitchen to set aside a croissant, and room service was informed that they would need to deliver the fresh croissant upon request.

This level of teamwork between different departments in the hotel was simply magical. All participants were aligned on the end objective – customer satisfaction. Everyone was fully clear about their individual roles in achieving this goal. No prizes for guessing where the Wynn family prefers to stay on all their vacations since then!

***

C] Quick Hacks:

- **Team Charter**: Depending on the situation, an explicit (or at least implicit) team charter that contains the following items is of great help:
    - End objective – why are we all here? What is the eventual goal?

- Individual roles & expectations
- Mode of working & interacting with you/amongst each other
- In case of a 'wow goal', it is critical to have a team discussion upfront and frequent check-ins subsequently.

A semi-professional athlete I know is training for a 100 km race. His team consists of a nutritionist, a gym trainer, a physiotherapist, and a running coach. All of them know his goal, his training plan and his personality. They all also have a common WhatsApp group where they exchange thoughts, changes to training plans and other issues.

In the corporate sector, team charters are more formal and structured, typically in the nature of project groups with clear KPIs, milestones, tracking mechanisms and meetings. However, managing large teams and ecosystems can also be a challenge in and of itself. Hence, the right team size is equally critical – too small and you have a risk of gaps; too large and you have the risk of friction and coordination challenges.

***

A Rolling Stone Gathers No Moss

Mick Jagger, Charlie Watts, Keith Richards, and Ronnie Wood, aka The Rolling Stones, are one of the most iconic bands ever (some would say they are no.2 after the Beatles in the all-time list!). They have played together for more than 50 years. However, they still recognize the importance of being one team – staying together, defining team norms, ironing out differences, and most importantly, practising together.

They understand that for excellence to become a habit, you need to define a shared approach to working together as a team, no matter how many years you have been together.

Before every tour, the band typically commits two months to rehearsing. They appreciate the opportunity to reconnect with their collective rhythms. The practice enables the band to perform with almost telepathic communication when their tour actually begins.

Richards says that he knows exactly what's happening by simply watching Watts' left hand. If the tempo ever drags, one glance from Richards to Wood speaks volumes. Together, they will then step up the pace. The Stones' success comes from each member having a distinctive yet complementary role. Richards is their spiritual leader, Watts the band's backbone, Wood the mediator, and Jagger controls everything like a chief executive.

Each band member is a talent in his own right, but it is their chemistry that works best. Being part of the Rolling Stones remains the best way for each member to achieve their individual goals – hence, the Stones are still together, despite it being very easily possible for each member to branch out on his own like so many other bands have!

***

> *"Alone we can do so little; together we can do so much."* (Helen Keller)
>
> *"Talent wins games, but teamwork and intelligence win championships."* (Michael Jordan)
>
> *"If I have seen further, it is by standing on the shoulders of giants."* (Isaac Newton)
>
> *"No one can whistle a symphony. It takes a whole orchestra to play it."* (H.E. Luccock)

9. Restraint

A] Core Idea: Unless we discipline our emotions, feelings, and thoughts, it is unlikely that we can achieve anything. Self-control is required to attain any goal. When the Nile is controlled appropriately, for instance, Egypt can turn into a fertile plain. But when it is uncontrolled, the same river destroys the land.

A goal of say, fitness requires us to stay away from eating certain things or from lounging around without exercise. The goal of building one's own business needs so many sacrifices in terms of declined vacations, reduced time with family, lesser rest and possibly, not pursuing other passions at the same time. As Michael Phelps put it, *"I never did anything that normal children did when I was small because I was so focused on becoming the Olympian Phelps. Yes, I missed out on my childhood but that was necessary to become what I am today."*

B] Points to Note:

1. Restraint is all about saying NO. This could be saying NO to a casual request to meet for drinks from your work colleague simply because you want to spend quality time with your family before your kids go to sleep. It can also mean refusing someone's request to run an errand when you have something to do to meet your aims. As runners know well, being able to run marathons involve lots of refusals: no partying late, no eating junk food, no drinking too much before a long run, saying no to late night movies...the list is endless.

2. Restraint is also about inflexible commitment – not swaying from your chosen path. If an examination requires you to put in 12 hours of study, then you have to do the 12 hours. This will be at the cost of everything else – from socialising, exercising, relaxing – everything that is not studying. But here is the thing: you cannot do what you WANT to do unless you have done what you NEED to do. That commitment to yourself and your goals must come above everything else.

3. Restraint is a refusal to do those things that could make you slip up. Remember, 'small slips can sink ships' – so once you swerve away from the path, it could be a dangerous slippery slope of no return!

4. Even minor deviations from the path can result in large deviations in output. Remember, a 1% change in flight path from Mumbai to Delhi will land you in Kolkata 3 hours later! Hence, restraint is about not giving in to the Devil's voice, which says, "Come on, this one time won't matter", or "Come on, a teeny-weeny bit is not going to make any difference."

C] Quick Hacks:

- **Digital Detox**: In today's age of digital-enabled distraction, it is impossible to focus on goals without the danger of getting sucked into thousands of WhatsApp messages, tweets, and Insta feeds. Plus, there is content on OTT platforms almost every day. If you have to prevent yourself from being distracted, you have to practice digital detox. Now, this could be of different types:

  - Continuous detox (up to 1 week), typically done in a retreat-type setting

- Daily detox – periods of no-digital engagement during specific periods (like the first hour after waking up or the last hour before sleeping)
- Earn the right to be online – you only engage digitally AFTER you have achieved your goal for the day!

o **The NO strategy**: Say NO to 80% of the requests that you get UNLESS they are aligned with your goal or it is something that you were going to do in any case. This could be:
  - Watching a movie
  - Going for a drink
  - Invitation to be a speaker

o This is especially valid if the request is for at least a month later. We often make the mistake of committing to things that are far away in the future since we feel that "we will most likely be free" at that time. However closer to the date, we realize that we are over-committed and regret accepting the invite. This is also called 'even elephants look tiny from a distance' framing. As the distance reduces, you realize the size of the elephant and the proportion of the blunder that you have committed. But now, it is too late to change since you will be met with a typical guilt-inducing response like, "But you had committed to this so many days/ weeks/ months in advance!" Or worse, "Who can we get at this last minute? We were depending on you."

o There are various strategies for saying NO, including:

- **Straight NO** – people get used to this over time and rarely ask you for superfluous things. They will respect your time, and hence, the chances of you getting distracted in future will be minimal.

- **Sandwich technique** – Like a sandwich, this NO has 3 layers. The 'first bread' says, "I would have really loved to….". The 'meat inside' then adds, "However, I am going to have to refuse given (rationale for refusal). The 'final bread layer' adds, "I hugely appreciate you asking me for this, and I am honoured. Next time…."

- **Delayed response** – some requests, especially those by folks NOT in your immediate circle of 'family and friends' as well as 'circle of importance', can be delayed for long, and then an 'Oops, I missed this… so sorry' can be done. No responses till the second follow-up and the request-maker usually gets the message.

o **'Deserve then Desire' mindset**: Say you are really tempted to eat that piece of chocolate, but your current goal is to reduce weight. You have tried resisting, but all you can think of is that piece of chocolate. In such a case, set an interim goal AFTER which you can have the chocolate. So, you can put a criterion that, "Only after I reduce another 1.5 kgs will I allow myself to eat the chocolate". This way, you build restraint while also comforting your mind that denial is not indefinite.

> *"Practice restraint over the following if you want to be a great man – appetite, sleep, lust and anger."* (Pythagoras)
>
> *"Your goals are not determined by what you will do but by what you will NOT do on that journey."* (Anonymous)
>
> *"One's greatest challenge is to control oneself – not others."* (Buddha)
>
> *"It is the failing of youth not to be able to restrain its own violence."* (Seneca)

10. Fear

A］ Core idea: In life, our personal fears are what hold us back the most – they prevent us from performing to our fullest potential. Unfortunately, most of our fears are never realized, and yet, in our own heads, they create a personal hell for us, which torments us and holds us back from greatness.

B］ Points to Note:

1. Research talks of 4 primary fears:
   a. Fear of public speaking – Socrates was the first to mention this more than 2000 years ago. Even today, this ranks as the no.1 fear – interesting!
   b. Fear of death – subsumed within this is the fear of the unknown since no one really knows what happens after we die.
   c. Fear or failure (and subsequent rejection)
   d. Fear of insecurity – this could be various types, including physical (e.g., poor health, impending illness), financial (bankruptcy, inadequacy to fulfil basic needs), social (e.g., being accepted into a cohort)

In this context, we are only going to focus on the fear of failure since that relates directly to our achievement of goals and dreams.

Fear Transformation

2. FEAR = **Fantasized Experience Appearing Real**. The main thing with Fear is that it is real, at least to its beholder. Others may often look at the same situation and wonder why the protagonist is 'scared' when he/she has so much experience, money, track record, etc.

3. FEAR = **Forget Everything & Run**. This is an evolutionary response at its core, generated by the amygdala that has helped us to survive on Earth. Hence, when faced with a stressor (i.e., an object that generates fear), we will either:

   a. Fight it (if we believe we are superior) OR

   b. Flight (if we can't face it) OR

   c. Freeze (just paralyzed with terror)

Our main focus has to be to turn Fear, as defined in (3), into **Face Everything & Rise** – a new definition of Fear.

***

This is a story of a person dreaming in his house. He sees himself walking into a rainforest. He hears a sound and looks behind. To his surprise, he sees a tiger. Naturally, out of fear, he starts running. The tiger also starts chasing him. He realizes he can't run too far and quickly climbs up a tree. The tiger follows him and waits below the tree.

Now, gasping for breath, the man thinks of settling here and moving up further. But when he looks up, a poisonous cobra is lying coiled above, waiting to bite him. His fear doubles. He tries to jump to the branches of the next tree, but unfortunately, that tree happens to be next to a cliff overlooking a valley.

So, he decides to stay where he is. Now, he listens to another creaking sound coming from the branch of the same tree where he is sitting. Due to his weight, the branch is breaking. Now, his fear triples.

He cannot go up because of the cobra, and he cannot come down because of the tiger. Nor can he move to the side since there is a cliff, and nor can he continue to stay put since the branch is cracking under his weight. What would you do if you were in this situation?

?

?

?

JUST WAKE UP!!!

Moral: We are sleeping and dreaming. Hence, it is better to wake up since the fear is solely in our minds. Ninety per cent of our fears never come true; the ten per cent that do were never in our control in any case.

***

C] **Quick Hacks**:

- **Scaled repetitive exposure (also known as exposure therapy)**: Do whatever you are most afraid of doing and increase its intensity in a gradual manner. For example, you might be scared of asking your boss for a salary increase. As per this technique, you would conquer this fear in 3 steps:

    - Step 1: Practice asking for a raise from a friendly person (not your boss) and play out the scenario in multiple ways with multiple people, as required.

    - Step 2: Practice asking your boss for something else that will lead to a debate/conflict. This will prepare you for a heated discussion with your boss.

    - Step 3: After repeating steps 1 and 2 enough number of times, the 'fear of what if...' will go away, leaving you finally ready to ask your boss for the raise.

- **Irrevocable commitment declaration**: Sometimes, due to fear, we are unable to commit to a goal, say running a marathon. We come up with enough excuses as to why we won't be able to do it. In this hack, you undertake an act(s) of irrevocable commitment to the goal, which could include:

    - Signing up for the marathon and letting enough people know about it

    - Paying for a coach and buying new shoes

    - Putting in an application for a 2 day leave for recovery after the marathon

- Telling your wife/friends not to allow you to do your favourite thing until you have achieved your goal
- **Prayer:** Religion has long proposed prayer as an effective means of overcoming fear. "God will take care of you if you hand over your fears to him", propound most reglions and religious leaders and gurus. This does work for some and is a very powerful means if it works for you.

> *"I never do anything out of fear – I do everything despite fear."* (Abraham Lincoln)
>
> *"A hero is not somebody who is not afraid of the demon, he is just a few minutes braver than others, long enough to scare the demon away."* (Anonymous)
>
> *"The only thing we have to fear is fear itself."* (Franklin D. Roosevelt)
>
> *"Trace your fear, grace your fear and erase your fear."* (Anonymous)

11. Roll with the Punches – Adapt & Evolve, Evolve & Adapt

A] Core idea: You can have an amazing plan, a structure, a routine, and a well-defined calendar with milestones that track your progress towards the achievement of your goals. This is essential, and without it, you are leaving the goal to chance. However, no matter who you are, what your goal is and how meticulous you may be in your planning, THINGS WILL GO WRONG. Or, at the very least, there will be changes and shifts that you had not anticipated.

It is when this happens that you need to absorb the impact of such unforeseen events, make your assessment, and then continue in your efforts towards the goal:

B] Points to Note:

1. All plans need to have some degree of flexibility – if plans are too rigid and regimented such that they do not allow for even the smallest changes, then that is exactly what will happen – the plan will have to be discarded in the face of 'life'. This is also one of the reasons why diets have cheat days!

2. The key is to be able to analyse the impact of the changes on the plan itself. For example, does the plan have to be modified marginally? Significantly? Or thrown into the dustbin entirely? If you had a goal of, say, doing the Ironman and a week before the event, you got into an accident that puts your

foot in plaster, which is a major shift, and it necessitates shifting your goal post entirely by going back to the drawing board. However, the fact that you could not practice for a few days due to excessive travel or workload is no reason to change the goal. All it needs is recommitting and modifying your workouts for the next few days.

3. At the end of this adaptation, the crux is to keep going and not stop. Yes, the changes may require shifts in the plan, but what must not change is your goal itself and your resolve to reach it.

C] Quick Hacks:

o **Damage Assessment:** Any shift or sudden occurrence should be mapped on a 2-dimensional matrix as shown below,

Damage Assessment Approach

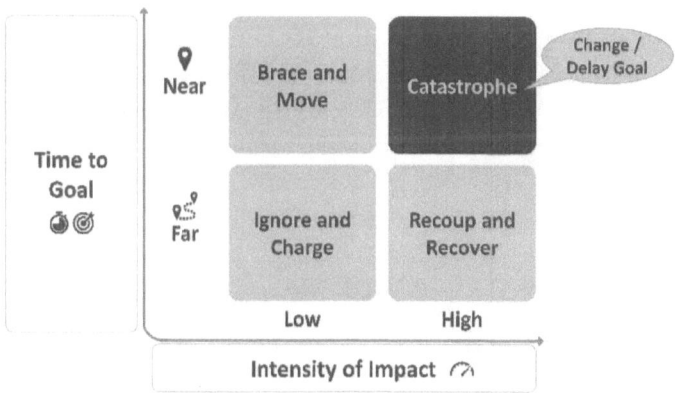

- The X-axis is the intensity of the impact that the change will have on your schedule, and the Y-axis is the proximity to the goal time. The higher the impact, the more changes are needed, especially as the goal 'date' approaches. In this scheme of things, a catastrophe will have a very high impact, occurring very close to the goal date. A minor flutter will be something that has a lower impact, occurring with adequate time from the date of the goal itself.

o **The 'Why' Mindset:** This hack is not featured in the motivation or the meditation section since it is a recommitment to the *reason* you started pursuing that goal in the first place. If and when you dither on the path of goal achievement, it is absolutely essential to step back and re-analyse why you started the journey in the first place. This can be done in several ways:

- You can meditate for fifteen minutes every day, visualising yourself before you begin working toward your goal, where you stand today, and how you will feel after the goal is achieved. Keep repeating to yourself why this goal matters so much to you. Tell yourself that despite everything, the GOAL IS THE ONLY THING THAT MATTERS.

- Write down the one primary reason why you set out to achieve the goal on the first day – write this not in one sentence but as a paragraph. The next day, read this paragraph and again, write down the reasons behind your goal on the next page. Repeat this process for 21 days. Your mind will then be firm and clear about its reasons, and it will have built its own narrative about why you need to be committed to that goal.

***

Don't Quit (John Greenleaf Whittier)

When things go wrong as they sometimes will,

When the road you're trudging seems all uphill.

When the funds are low and the debts are high,

And you want to smile, but you have to sigh.

When care is pressing you down a bit,

Rest if you must, but don't you quit.

Life is queer with its twists and turns,

As everyone of us sometimes learns.

And many a fellow turns about,

When he might have won had he stuck it out.

Don't give up though the pace seems slow,

You may succeed with another blow.

Often the goal is nearer than

It seems to a faint and faltering man.

Often the struggler has given up,

When he might have captured the victor's cup.

And he learned too late when the night came down,

How close he was to the golden crown.

Success is failure turned inside out,

The silver tint of the clouds of doubt.

And you never can tell how close you are,

It may be near when it seems afar.

So, stick to the fight when you're hardest hit,

It's when things seem worst that you mustn't quit.

***

> *"Everyone has a plan till they get punched in the face." (Mike Tyson)*
>
> *"Winners never quit, quitters never win." (Anonymous)*
>
> *"Develop success from failures. Discouragement and failure are two of the surest stepping stones to success." (Dale Carnegie)*

12. Time Management

A] **Core idea:** Everything about your life and the goals that you seek to achieve is about using your time wisely. Time is the only currency that you have in equal measure to every other human and animal on the planet. We may have differing abilities, opportunities, genetics, riches and potential, but we are fully equal in terms of the time we have on our hands every day. All of us have the same 24 hours each day for 365 days of the year. Once we spend even one second of that time, it is gone, never to return. Hence, in order to achieve our goals, we need to spend our time purposefully. Time does not wait. It will expend itself irrespective of what we are doing or not doing, as the case may be.

B] **Points to Note**:

1. Time is not just a physical concept – it is a man-made one. We can use this to divide our life into "chunks" (productive-unproductive, sleeping-waking, working-relaxing) or parts that we can utilize as per our choice.

2. How you spend your time is how you will live your life. Life is nothing but small chunks of time which are aggregated together. Moreover, your priorities are NOT a function of what you say but of how you spend your time. For example, you can say that mending your relationship with your partner is your priority. Indeed, you can shout this from the rooftops. But a mere look at your calendar will tell

you (and your partner!) whether you are serious about this or not.

   a. How much time did you spend with your partner?
   b. How did you spend that time – fighting or doing things together?
   c. Did you plan this time, or was it unplanned?
   d. Did you show up 'on time'? Were you focused during the time you were together or taking other calls, checking emails and posting stuff on social media?

3. Certain portions of time are essentially 'gone', or at the least, there is only so much you can do to optimize them, like sleep, eating time, time for bodily needs etc. However, there are at least 12-16 hours every day that you can focus on to determine what you want to do with your life!

***

Spare Time (Bertrand Russell)

Spare time to observe, it is to rectify mistakes.

Spare time to live, it is the pleasure of life.

Spare time to think, it is the source of wisdom.

Spare time for friendship, it is the root of happiness.

Spare time to work, it is the base of prosperity.

Spare time to admire, it is for others' encouragement.

Spare time to walk, it is the wealth for good health.

Spare time to play, it is for discipline and enthusiasm.

Spare time to live, it is the divine message for unity.

Spare time to watch, it is the inspiration towards nature.

Spare time to read, it is the foundation of knowledge.

Spare time for family, it is the foundation of humanity.

Spare time to pray, it is worship for purity of thoughts.

***

C] Quick Hacks:

- **The 'Urgent-Important' Matrix:** We spend our time doing lots of activities on a daily basis. All of them can be classified on a 2x2 matrix in terms of Important vs Urgent, as shown in the diagram below:

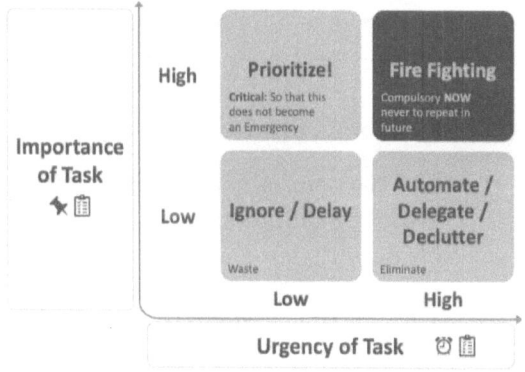

Quite a lot of the activities we do are in the 'Urgent + Important' zone — these can't be deferred or dodged. They are what I like to call "mission critical." For instance, if you are injured, then going to the doctor is both important *and* urgent.

Similarly, when you are surprised by a sudden review meeting, preparing for it becomes important *and* urgent. These are, however, emergency situations.

- Unfortunately, we also spend a lot of time in the 'Urgent but NOT Important' activity zone. These are 'firefights' that could have been avoided had one planned ahead of time. This includes paying bills at the last minute to avoid a cut-off of services or forgetting to prepare for a scheduled meeting and then pulling an all-nighter to prepare.

- The most critical zone is the 'Important but not Urgent' zone – the place where you focus on doing things that matter but are not required to be done immediately. Activities that will help you become a better professional and live a happier life are all in this zone. **However**, you can only spend time here IF you are not firefighting constantly!

- The last zone is 'neither Important nor Urgent' – you should not **spend** any time in this zone. Ideally, whatever activities are here should be delegated to someone else, denied or at least deferred. This is the WASTE ZONE.

o **Eat the Frog First**: As the popular book by this same name goes (author: Brian Tracy), every day, first do the things that you hate the most or are trying to avoid. That could range from having the difficult conversation with your subordinate that you have been avoiding or doing the intense workout you've been dreading. Our mind works in strange ways – when the "frog" is out of the way, you will feel that tons of time is suddenly available to do the things that you really enjoy doing.

o **5Ds**: All our tasks can be put into one of the 5 Ds as shown in the diagram below:

5Ds Of Time Management

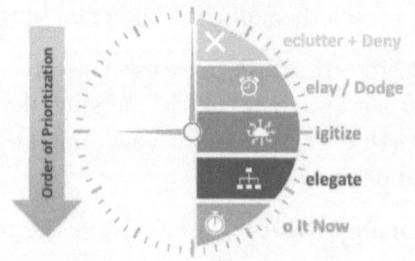

- De-clutter and DENY – This is the first D. Your 'task mountain' will have lots of tasks that may seem to drown you. However, when you step back and view them, you will realize that not all tasks need to be done by you. Moreover, not all need to be done now. Some don't need to be done at all

- Delay/ Dodge – Post denying, 50 per cent of the things you still have do will fall into this bracket. You don't need to accept all the invitations that come your way, for instance. You don't need to join the 'optional calls' or, for that matter, the after-work drinks that are so routine.

- Digitize – lots of tasks can be automated using a variety of tools, apps, and programs. This could be things like monitoring your health and setting reminders (including standing instructions for pesky bill payments that are routine).

- Delegate – tasks that are better, cheaper or faster to be done by someone else. Your time is NOT worth the effort it would take for these. If others don't know how to do these tasks, you can teach them once but don't do it again.

- Do it – If a task does not fall into one of the earlier Ds, then that is the stuff that is really worth every second of your time and needs to get done ASAP.

o **Optimizing Digital Time**: Given the plethora of 'amazing and spectacular' digital entertainment and engagement options we have today, we don't even realize how much time we spend across all platforms ranging from OTT to social media (WhatsApp, Insta). Here are my 5 favourite hacks:

- Select earlier what you want to see on Netflix/Amazon Prime/other platforms. This can be done using recommendations from friends or at the end of your earlier session. An average user spends 20-25 per cent of time scrolling through stuff that he/she never sees eventually, or at least not completely.

- Put timer locks on all devices – no more than say, two hours on social media.

- 'Digital-free' times – especially one hour before sleeping, one hour after waking up and during meals. This hack itself can help your productivity zoom like hell!

- Have a non-digital hobby/ passion – developing this and engrossing yourself in it will take away the time you have for a digital life. The reason this is effective (beyond the obvious benefits of the hobby) is that digital is like a never-ending maze – once you start going in, it is difficult to stop & pull out. It's better to avoid getting tempted rather than try and moderate the temptation.

***

Time Out For Today (Gerald Klein)

Today is here, I will start with a smile and resolve to be agreeable.

I will not criticize. I refuse to waste my valuable time.

Today has one aspect in which I know I am equal with all others-time.

All of us draw the same salary in seconds, minutes, and hours.

Today I will not waste my time because the minutes I wasted yesterday.

are lost as a vanquished thought.

Today I refuse to spend time worrying about what might happen – it usually doesn't.

I am going to spend time making things happen.

Today I am determined to study to improve myself,

for tomorrow I may be wanted, and I must not be found lacking.

Today I am determined to do the things that I should do.

I firmly determine to stop the things I should not do.

Today I begin by doing, and not wasting my time.

In one week, I will be miles beyond the person I am today.

Today I will not imagine what I would do if things were different.

They are not different. I will make success with what material I have.

Today I will stop saying, "If I had time…" I know I will never find time for anything.

If I want time, I must make it.

Today I will act towards other people as though this might be my last day on earth.

I will not wait for tomorrow. Tomorrow never comes.

✳✳✳

> *"Time isn't the main thing – it is the only thing." (Anonymous)*
>
> *"Time is what we want most but use worst." (Anonymous)*
>
> *"Once gone, even a second can't come back." (Ingvar Kamprad)*
>
> *"Manage your time or time will manage you!" (P J Caposey)*
>
> *"Life & Time are the world's best teachers. Life teaches us to make good use of time. Time teaches us the value of life." (Dr. Abdul Kalam)*

13. Energy Management

A] Core idea: It is not really time that we should manage but our energy. Yes, time is critical as a resource, as we have seen in the earlier chapter, but it is an artificial concept (sorry, Dr. Einstein). Who says a day needs to have only 24 hours? Who decreed that Saturday & Sunday are to be 'holy days? Man created the concept of what time to start work and what time to stop work. So, it is not actually time that we must focus on but our energies that enable us to make the best (or worst) use of the time we have at hand. Energy management is, thus, another way to live your life without being restricted by 'artificial time'. Will it matter if you take out time for your family but are too exhausted when you are with them to make any meaningful use of it?

B] Points to Note:

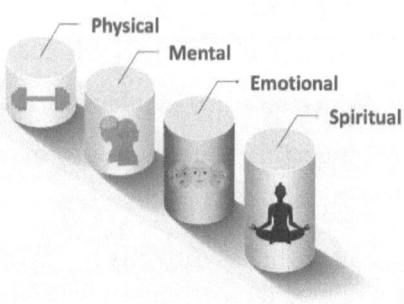

Cylinders of Energy

1. There are 4 energy cylinders that drive us as shown above, namely physical energy, mental energy, emotional energy and spiritual energy. Each cylinder enables us to use that specific energy for a certain period, after which the cylinder, like a battery, runs dry and needs to be recharged.
   a. Physical cylinder activities include everything that do with the body's energy levels and hence cover:
      i. Exercise
      ii. Sleep
      iii. Nutrition & hydration
   b. Mental cylinder activities include everything that requires the grey cells, including:
      i. Work (analysis, presentations, debates, discussions and decision-making)
      ii. Solving puzzles
      iii. Learning new skills
   c. Emotional cylinder activities include activities that involve feelings, such as:
      i. Spending time with friends and family
      ii. Watching a movie/ play
      iii. Interacting with people in a social setting
      iv. Listening to music
   d. Spiritual cylinder activities cover things that are generally to do with oneself, including:
      i. Meditation

ii. Going on walks alone

   iii. Journalling your thoughts

2. Every cylinder can be drained or recharged by doing more or less of the activities therein.

   a. Physical energy is drained when we keep working the body without proper rest & sleep. It can also be drained by eating (or drinking) lots of junk food. On the contrary, the physical energy cylinder is recharged with proper exercise, sleep and diet.

   b. Mental energy is drained when we keep working in the office for long hours – that's when we feel 'burnt out' and need a vacation or 'me time'. Mental energy is recharged after breaks, where brain fatigue is reduced due to play and leisure.

   c. Emotional energy is drained after lots of social interactions (ever heard of marriage season fatigue when both families need a break just to recover from the emotional intensities of the wedding?). However, we can also recharge the same cylinder by meeting friends, going out and building connections.

   d. Lastly, the spiritual energy cylinder is drained by neglect, especially in today's day and age when we have time for everything except ourselves. A morning meditation or a long afternoon spent reading a book alone can give us a much-needed dose of spiritual energy. Acts of kindness and gratitude are also beneficial for this purpose. Many religions emphasize activities like listening to scriptures, devotional songs (e.g., bhajans) and volunteering for this purpose.

3. If we keep drawing from a cylinder continuously, the cylinder, very similar to a battery, runs empty. Thus, the cylinders of energy need to be used in balance so that we can engage a particular one long enough to derive its full benefits but not so long that the energy starts depleting.

4. Energy blockers prevent us from using our cylinders in a balanced manner. More often than not, such blockers distract our energies into doing stupid & wasteful things. This is in line with Marie Kondo's philosophy of decluttering one's life so that one can be always in a flow state. Blockers include:

   a. Too many tasks to do without purpose.

   b. Articles strewn around the house/workplace, which defocus us.

   c. A busy social calendar but without purpose – these interactions will surely drain us!

C] Quick Hacks:

o **Energy Tracking**: Keep track of which cylinders you use during a day and week and for how long – develop a better understanding of when you feel low/ fatigued physically, mentally, emotionally or spiritually. After a few days of keeping track, you will understand your 'energy zones', i.e., how many cylinders are used and when, what are the optimal usage levels, what enables you to recharge a particular cylinder, etc.

> *"We are not physical beings expending energies but energy beings on Earth in a physical form. We are merely energy beings, having human experiences with the body."* (Dr. Wayne Dyer)
>
> *"Where attention goes, energy flows; Where intention goes, energy flows."* (James Redfield)
>
> *"Remember to park your car (body) in the SHED – Sleep, Hydrate, Exercise, Diet."* (Dr. Ajay Tamhane)

***

Of the different energy replenishers & drainers, I am going to focus on five replenishers that are extremely important for overall well-being, primarily with the objective of being able to achieve any goal that we want to seek, including:

13.A] Sleep:

A] Core idea: All of us need a basic 'minimum amount' of sleep for our bodies and brains to function properly. While scientists differ on the exact amount needed, most will arrive at a number between 6-8+ hours of sleep at night for an adult. If we sleep less than this 'minimum quota', our cognitive abilities and physical health, digestion, and emotional balance will be impaired.

Nature wants us to sleep for various reasons – anything that nature does not want us to do is eliminated over time due to the process of evolution (e.g., tails in humans, appendix use). However, all animals (including single-celled ones) sleep – hence it is safe to conclude that sleep is CRITICAL, not optional, for life on earth.

Not allowing someone to sleep is a form of the worst torture, often done to prisoners to get them to break down.

Unfortunately, many of us seem to take delight in subjecting ourselves to a similar torture voluntarily and lovingly on a regular basis. What an irony!

B] Points to Note:

1. All of us, genetically, are either 'owls' (those who sleep late and wake up late) or 'larks' (those who sleep early and wake up early). It is important to understand one's biorhythm and determine what works for you. It is futile to stay up late as a lark and equally useless to try and sleep early as an owl. We are just not 'cut out for it.'

2. Sleep is not uniform. There are several stages of sleep, the most important ones being deep sleep (high-quality sleep) and REM sleep (a state wherein our subconscious mind opens up). The endeavour is to try to get a deep sleep as soon as possible.

3. If we stay in a state of perpetual sleep deficit, the harmful effects on our bodies are irreversible. On the contrary, if we get good sleep, it will manifest in the superior functioning of our brain and body.

4. Doing the 'weekend sleep warrior routine', i.e., staying awake at odd hours and then trying to compensate over weekends, does not work except as a one-off exception, i.e., you have an important assignment and have to stay awake for it, for which you make up by sleeping a lot when the strain of the assignment is over.

5. Scientists have tried to dig deeper and coin terms like 'polyphasic sleep' (where you sleep multiple times during the day and sleep much less at night) – and yes, there are several historical figures whose

sleeping patterns are bizarre by 'normal standards' (e.g., 30-minute nap every 4 hours, 3 naps of 20 minutes during the day and only 3-4 hours at night). While such sleeping techniques have worked for a few, for the vast majority, 6-8 hours at night is the best solution.

C] Quick Hacks:

- **4-3-2-1-0.5 rule - AVOID:**
  - Caffeine intake at least 4 hours prior
  - Vigorous exercise at least 3 hours prior
  - Food & alcohol at least 2 hours prior
  - Water at least 1 hour prior (reduce having to wake up to pee at night)
  - Digital light at least 30 mins prior (i.e., no T.V, phones, iPad)

- **Sleep routine**: Develop a routine, if possible. Sleep and wake up at the same time. Create the right atmosphere & ritual in the bedroom in the 30–60 minute window prior to sleep, which can include:
  - Soothing music
  - A warm bath
  - Meditation
  - Aromas/ scents
  - Massage – self or partner
  - Ambient lighting or darkness – use of eye masks and ear plugs

- An optimal mattress & pillow – there are tons of products out there advertising the best sleep products. Feel free to try whatever works!

○ **Siesta**: The Spanish practice of an afternoon siesta is a powerful one since it enables a mini reset during the day. It is credited to be one of the reasons that Mediterranean folks live longer and healthier lives than others.

○ **Catnapping** is another technique that busy people use to refresh themselves. Salvador Dali had a unique technique for catnapping. He would hold a spoon in one hand and sleep on a chair. Below the spoon was kept a plate – as soon as Dali started dozing off, the spoon would fall on the plate and make a clanging noise, waking him up. He would do this 3-4 times during a session and wake up totally fresh for his next tasks.

> *"Sleep is the single most important thing that we can do to reset our brain and body health each day. Look at babies – they sleep so well and are always happy. "(Matt Walker)*
>
> *"Sleep is the best meditation." (Dalai Lama)*
>
> *"A good laugh and a long sleep are the best cures in a doctor's book." (Irish proverb)*

13.B Exercise:

Note: The pointers here are for general well-being and NOT if you have a specific (or even crazy) goal of, say, weight reduction or running 100 marathons in 100 days!

A] **Core Idea:** We need a healthy body to achieve our goals – no one ever did anything meaningful from a hospital bed. There is a strong link between the mind and the body. In fact, the mind and the body are a part of the same integrated system.

The optimal exercise combo is one that gives you the **5S** of fitness, namely:

o   **S**trength – you want to remain strong for as much of your life as possible.

o   **S**tamina – this refers to your cardiovascular fitness. A healthy heart that can pump blood as efficiently as possible.

o   **S**peed – refers to the explosive power in your muscles.

o   **S**uppleness – refers to the flexibility that becomes important with age as we start losing the elasticity in our muscles, ligaments, and tendons.

o   **S**kill – refers to the dexterity with which you can do various tasks. It is also associated with hand-eye-muscle coordination.

B] **Points to Note:**

1.   While we don't need to work out like elite athletes, a certain minimum level is critical to ensure a well-functioning body that can enable us to do whatever we want, whether that is an office assignment that needs us to travel to all places at odd hours or appear for a competitive exam that entails studying 10+ hours every day.

2.   Most people make excuses to avoid workouts. Some of the most common ones are:

i. "I don't have time for exercise" – *if you don't have time for health, you will find time for sickness!*

ii. "There is no gym near me" - *you don't need a gym to work out – just the desire to exercise and your own body.*

iii. "I am too tired by the time I get home" – *what about working out before going to work? What about 15 minutes at lunchtime? What about cycling to work and back? What about climbing stairs at work instead of taking the elevator?*

iv. "I hate sweaty bodies around me" – *so do yoga, swimming or running on the roads or in a park!*

C] Quick Hacks:

o **The GOAT(s) of exercise**: If you could do only 1 exercise and had only 15 minutes, just do

- Western version: 100 burpees OR
- Eastern version: 100 sun salutations
- Either of these exercises is sufficient to give you a full-body workout without the need for any equipment or space. The burpee is essentially a combination of a push-up, squat jump and mountain climber, whereas the sun salutation (simplest version) takes you through 8-10 yoga postures. These are ideal exercises from a 'Return on Time spent' perspective.

o **Short run:** If you are into running, a 5 km run is the best workout you can do within 45 minutes. The 'runner's high' that you will experience will carry you throughout the day. For a worst-case scenario, walk for thirty minutes three or four times a week.

Even this amount of exercise will give you the majority of 'base benefits' needed.

o **Variety** is the spice of life! Try to do a few different things every week to prevent boredom. Choose one of each:

- Strength development (e.g., gym, weights)
- Stamina building (e.g., running, sports like football, badminton, dance)
- Stretching (e.g., yoga, Pilates)

This diversification not only prevents boredom but also ensures that the benefits from the workout don't plateau. Try to do at least one of the activities as a group/ team effort to also gain social benefits.

o **Sports or relaxation massage**: Get a massage at least once a month if you can. This helps to release knots and tension from your muscles. The type of massage really depends on your preference and context; it could be soothing and relaxing if you are stressed or a deep-tissue one if you have indulged in intense physical activity or even some good-old Thai stretching if you are too stiff in the joints.

> *"Exercises are a tribute to what your body can do – not a punishment for what you ate." (Dr. Ajay Tamhane)*
>
> *"You are only 1 workout away from a good mood." (Anonymous)*
>
> *"Exercise not only changes your body but also your mind, attitude and mood." (BKS Iyengar)*
>
> *"Exercising is so difficult when you HAVE to and so easy when you WANT to." (Dean Karnazes, ultramarathon runner)*
>
> *"Do something today that your future self will thank you for – Exercise." (Dr. Ajay Tamhane)*
>
> *"Take damn good care of your body – it is the only place that you have to live in." (Internet meme)*
>
> *"This month's exercise is next month's health." (Internet meme)*

13.C: Nourishment/ Nutrition

A] **Core Idea**: In the conventional sense, when we talk of nourishment, our idea is that of the food we eat and the beverages we consume. While this is the primary topic of focus, there are two other sources of nourishment that we need to be mindful of, namely:

1] The various other sensory inputs that we get (or are given) – could include the sights we see, the sounds we hear, and the things we touch. While from a 'pure scientific sense', these are not nourishments, from a spiritual standpoint, these are equally important inputs that can either help or harm us.

2] Feelings, whether individual or collective, also go towards nourishing (or otherwise). So, if we are surrounded by an angry mob, we are most likely going to feel angry. Similarly, if we are in a highly motivated environment, our 'soul' or 'psyche' gets nourished accordingly.

B] Points to Note:

1. Food becomes us – essentially, whatever we eat becomes a part of our bodies through the processes of digestion and subsequent absorption. Hence, it is true that 'we are what we eat'. A diet full of junk food will not only weaken us physically but also mentally.

2. Similarly, what we consume through our other senses plays an equally important role in becoming 'us'. If we surround ourselves with positive environments, we grow both physically & mentally, thereby enabling the achievement of our goals.

C] Quick Hacks:

- **Food**:
  - Eat as much natural food as possible. Anything that comes out of a packet or tetra pack, or bottle is NOT natural.

  - Follow some type of fasting schedule – this could be intermittent or skipping 1 meal a week. There is no need to be extreme, but this fasting detox is the key to a stronger physiological system, health and longevity. Today, there are tons of 'fasting protocols' available, ranging from Intermittent Fasting (IF) to 'day a week fast'. Do whatever suits you but doing at least one on a regular basis is critical.

- Always eat up to 80% of your appetite.

- Social drinking is okay, but anything more is dangerous.

- Understand what foods are unsuitable for you, either because of their reaction to you or your inherent disposition. All of us are allergic to certain foods and get affected differently.

- Reduce the acidic content in food as much as possible. Our body is designed to be alkaline, and hence, alkaline foods are to be eaten as much as possible.

- Chew properly – this is the primary source of various digestive disorders.

- Pray before starting your meal – the mindset that you eat with determines a lot of your body's chemical reactions.

- Cheating is almost mandatory, atleast once a week – the body should be left with no cravings. It is not possible for us to resist cravings beyond a point. Hence, we have to succumb to temptation in the right manner. Scientists call this the 'temptation threshold' – if you try to resist everything, then you will fall prey to something at the worst possible moment. It is better to create these moments proactively. There is merit in comfort food. When you really need something badly, it is okay to indulge in your favourite comfort food. Just don't make it a habit.

- Keep a log of your food intake – you will be shocked at the amount of crap we feed ourselves without knowing it.
- While there are lots of recommendations on vitamins and supplements (including cod liver oil, Omega 3 capsules, zinc-magnesium-calcium, protein supplements like whey and BCAA, etc), you should always consult a doctor before starting this and not just keep popping pills or gulping mixtures.

- **Sensory inputs**:
  - Have good music playlists – a) something that charges you up and b) something that soothes you.
  - Always have a list of 5 new books that you want to read that are highly recommended. Read 1 good book every month.
  - Listen to inspiring podcasts – we don't need depressing advertisements and social media prompts that make us feel miserable.

- **Feelings**:
  - No.1 rule – surround yourselves with positive people. Remember, you are the average of the 10 people you keep most company with.
  - At least take 10 minutes every day to think of what you are feeling and why. Journalling will help.
  - If you feel that an atmosphere is getting toxic, EXIT immediately. Even if you don't actively participate in the discussions, your mind will

keep thinking of this long after the discussion is over. Nip the mischief in the bud!

> *"One cannot think well, love well, sleep well, if one has not dined well." (Virginia Woolf)*
>
> *"Breakfast like a king, lunch like a prince and dinner like a pauper." (Old English saying)*
>
> *"Let food be thy medicine and medicine be thy food." (Hippocrates)*
>
> *"Tell me what you eat, and I will tell you who you are." (Jean Anthelme Brillat-Savarin)*
>
> *"Food for the body is not enough. There must be food for the soul." (Dorothy Day)*
>
> *"A crust eaten in peace is better than a banquet partaken in anxiety." (Aesop)*
>
> *"Exercise is King. Nutrition is Queen. Put them together and you've got a kingdom." (Jack La Lanne)*

13.D Brain Fitness:

A] **Core Idea**: To achieve any goals, the most important organ, i.e., the brain, needs to be 'fit.' Just as you exercise to build strength, it is possible to exercise the brain to build its fitness.

The earlier theory of brain development claimed that our brains develop only until we are five or six years old. By this time, our neural networks have been formed. Beyond this age, it is impossible to see dramatic improvements in brain capabilities. However, subsequent research in neuroscience has led us to conclude that our brains are capable of neuroplasticity, i.e., the brain keeps getting moulded (through the folds) if we keep actively exercising it.

B] Points to Note:

1. From a developmental standpoint, there are 2 parts to the brain – the left brain (logical thinking) and the right brain (creativity). Both need to be worked on in different ways.

2. The essence of brain development is to activate as many neural networks as possible in both hemispheres of the brain so that it is forced to do different things consciously. Diversity pushes development, whereas familiarity leads to stagnation.

C] Quick Hacks:

- **Left Brain Development**:
  - Solve various types of puzzles (crosswords, sudoku, kakuro, lateral thinking)
  - Play boardgames, especially ones involving strategy & multi-step thinking (e.g. Catan, Risk, Sherlock Holmes Consulting Detective, Project L, Battleship).
  - Say numbers backwards from 100 to 1 consecutively, then with gaps of 3, e.g., 100-97-94, then gaps of 7, then gaps of 9). If you get a number wrong, start back from 100.
  - Try to memorize an entire deck of cards – there are various memory techniques available for doing this (e.g., building a memory palace and assigning characters to the cards).

- Play games of logic like chess or bridge.
- Try to recite people's names and phone numbers backwards (I am NAHSOT ENAHMAT, 5166060289).
- Try to remember what you ate for breakfast, lunch and dinner yesterday, then 2 days prior, then 3 days and so on... Can you go a week back?

o **Right Brain Development**:
- Learn to play a musical instrument, a new dance form or a new sport that involves hand-eye coordination (e.g., badminton, tennis, table tennis)
- Take up a completely different hobby from what you do in your 'main work area (e.g., cooking, gardening, lego, origami)
- Read about 1 topic that you have no clue about or interest in (e.g., the marriage rituals of the Mayan civilisation, the origins of World War 1 or the Darwinian theory of evolution)
- Do something that involves balance (e.g., walking on a thin surface, jumping on a trampoline)
- In a crowd, look at random people and try to come up with a hypothesis on their 'life' – who they are, what their profession is, what their family situation is etc.

- General Tips:
  - Sleep is a key driver of brain fitness. Hence, any sleep deficiency will result in putting checks on the extent of development that happens.
  - Change your dominant hand (or leg) for an activity. For example, if you are used to brushing with your right hand, brush with your left hand for a change. If you are used to tying your left shoelace first, switch occasionally.

Doing the same thing over and over in exactly the same manner reduces the brain's strength. The brain always looks for shortcuts and tries to reduce the number of neurons involved in a task. So, keep changing the way you do routine things – for example, if you always tie your right shoe first, do your left one as a starter. If you always wear your watch on the left hand, try it on the right. Change how you introduce yourself over the phone as an exercise for a whole day – it is DAMN TOUGH, though it looks easy.

> *"Brain power improves by brain use; just as bodily strength grows with exercise." (Dr. Ajay Tamhane)*
>
> *"The purpose of the body is to carry the brain around and not the other way round." (Internet meme)*
>
> *"Wonder why there are so many gyms devoted to the body and hardly any to the brain? The brain uses more than 40% of the energy in the body – one would have thought that this fact alone would have led to some brain development centres, courses and methods." (Lancelot Ware, founder of the Mensa Society)*

13.E. Meditation:

Note: Meditation could have been put as a sub-element within any of the chapters (say, stress management, visualization, or even happiness). However, given how critical it is for success as well as for life in general, I wanted to cover it as a separate element.

A] Core Idea: So much has been said and written over the ages about the benefits of meditation that this is not the place to repeat it. Nothing fundamentally will be learned by the reader. There is only one thing that I will propose here. Anything can be meditation, and meditation can be anything, provided that there are four things that are ultimately achieved:

a) Having the intention to meditate and setting up the activity as such.

b) Concentration on "something" – this could be a chant, a voice, a focal point, or a thought.

c) Minimization of other thoughts. If you ask the yogis, they will emphasise the complete elimination of other thoughts, but I think this is too much for a beginner.

d) The synchronization of mind & body (and if you are a believer, then the soul, too) in performing the task at hand.

As long as the above is achieved on the 'input side', you are definitely going to get all the benefits of meditation in terms of a sense of calm, centredness, reduction in body metrics like blood pressure and breath, as well as entering into higher states of consciousness.

My personal experience is that meditating for as little as 10 minutes each day gives immense benefits. Folks do it for a lot longer, even hours and days in retreats, which is, of course, more impactful. But the key is to be regular for even a little time rather than irregular for large periods.

B] Points to Note:

1. There is no need to sit in a lotus pose or lie down and relax in order to meditate. Of course, certain body postures and ambient environmental conditions definitely aid in meditation. In fact, meditating in the same spot over time builds a connection with the location that helps to accelerate the process.

2. There is also no need to stay still while meditating. Have you ever heard of 'walking meditation' or even 'flow meditation'? Endurance athletes like marathoners and mountaineers mention being in a meditative state where they feel 'one with themselves' as they are doing an intense physical activity. This is no different from the 'lying down guided meditation' that one sees in various apps or in monasteries and meditation retreats.

3. There is no need for meditation to have any religious or spiritual connotation. If you are already religious or spiritual, a meditative technique aligned to your ideology will be easier and more impactful for you.

4. There are more than 50+ meditation techniques since I last checked, including transcendental meditation, Kundalini meditation, guided hypnotic meditation, Tummo meditation and so on.

Experiment with a few before you figure out what you like and what works for you.

C❑ **Quick Hacks**:

o **My favourite meditations**:

- Breath meditation: This relies on concentrating on the inflow and outflow of breath. It can be done for anywhere between 10 minutes to over an hour, and practitioners swear by its rejuvenating properties.

- Aum meditation: This relies on chanting the primordial sound, Aum, in different ways so as to focus attention on exhalation while chanting Aum. This technique is closely aligned with Hindu and Buddhist religions, but not exclusively.

- Boxing meditation: Yes, this is ironically, one of the most peaceful ones for me. The body is vigorously hitting the punching bag or sparring, and your mind is just focused on the action of hitting, dodging and moving. At the end of an intense boxing session, I am sweaty and breathless, but I feel calm inside. It is almost as if the mind has been on a relaxing vacation! After all, it was unable to think of the 12,456 thoughts that it normally does at the same time. There is only one thought – *how to avoid getting hit by your opponent OR how to hit the opponent/bag!*

The key is to do whatever meditation suits you DAILY – that's the only way it will have the most impact on your life. Another option is to meditate on a reactive basis, i.e., when you are feeling stressed or angry. This is not as effective as the earlier option, but it's still better than doing nothing.

> *"Brilliant things happen inside calm minds." (Dalai Lama)*
>
> *"Learn to calm the mind and you will always be happy." (Paramahansa Yogananda)*
>
> *"Quiet the mind and the soul will speak." (Ma Jaya Sati Bhagvati)*
>
> *"Meditation is allowing what is – being honest with oneself without any filters." (Dr. Goenka)*
>
> *"Meditation is a vital way to purify and quiet the mind, thereby rejuvenating the body." (Deepak Chopra)*
>
> *"You should sit in meditation for 20 min a day; unless you're too busy, then you should sit for an hour." (Old Zen saying)*

14. Stress Management

A] Core Idea: We all get stressed – no surprises there. Moreover, we all know (or think we know) that stress is bad. Stress causes so many disorders, diseases and ailments. It is the root of so many physiological as well as psychological issues that we are almost "afraid of stress". It is so common to hear the words, "Oh, I am so stressed," or "I need to relax/ chill out so that I don't get stressed further!"

However, stress is not all that bad – in fact, a certain optimum stress level is critical for peak performance. If you were never worried about your goals, or if you never felt even a little anxious, you would not have been able to perform to your fullest potential. Hence, we need to distinguish between 'distress' (bad stress) and 'eustress' (positive stress). We need the latter, but not so much as it turns into the former. There is a spectrum or continuum that we need to be aware of and not let our stress exceed our eustress levels.

B] Points to Note:

1. Stress is the non-specific response of a body to any demand made upon it for change. It is non-specific because we don't know how the body will react – will it make the heartbeat faster? Will it upset the stomach or cause the head to hurt? It could be all of these and something more.

2. Stress is a natural evolutionary reaction triggered by the amygdala to a situation to which we are personally attached. As a layman, one is never

stressed by a news item that reads, "XX movie is a disaster" – however, the producer of that movie will be damn stressed on reading the same item!

3. Hence, the fact that *you* are stressed indicates your involvement in the situation. The level of stress is directly proportional to your involvement.

4. The other aspect of stress is assessment of your adequacy/ capability to deal with the situation. A world chess champion is never stressed when he is playing a beginner – though he is involved in the situation, he knows that victory is assured. One is worried when one feels uncertain of the outcome and one's ability to influence the outcome.

***

Once, there lived a wise man who never stressed about anything or anyone. He was always serene and composed with no worries and concerns.

One day, his son fell down from a tree and broke his leg. The doctor's prognosis was the worst possible: the little boy would never be able to walk properly. When his family came to the wise man to console him, they found him laughing and playing cards. Shocked, they asked him, "Aren't you worried about your son?"

"Will worrying help my son?" The wise man responded, "If it will, then yes, I will start worrying from tomorrow, nay today!"

After a few days, all the young men in the village were asked to join the army to fight against the enemy. Only the wise man's son was excused, given his disability. Again, the family came to ask the wise man, "Aren't you worried that all the other young boys will get fame, glory and riches as a result of fighting the King? Your son will be left behind?"

"Will worrying help?" The man replied again, "If it will, I will start tomorrow. Meanwhile, my son and I will make special weapons for the young men who are joining the army."

A year later, the war was over. The families of those from the village whose sons had been killed in the battle were compensated handsomely. Those who had survived were returning with pensions. Again, the family members approached the wise man, "Aren't both of you worried that you will remain poor while others around you will be rich?"

This time, the son (who was still limping) responded, "Will worrying help? Actually, I am happy about this news since our village will now become even more prosperous. All the various ventures that I launched in the last year, as the only young founder in the village, will become even more successful".

***

C] Quick Hacks:

- **30 minute worry and active relaxation rule:** Often, the more you agonize over a situation, the worse it becomes, and your thoughts (and actions) are the main reasons behind it. The 30-minute rule says that for 30 minutes, worry as much as you want about the stressors at hand, write down the worst-case scenario and feel free to stress yourself out. At the end of this period, do something actively that takes your mind totally off the situation. It could be a boxing session (you have to be so focused to avoid getting hit that you can't think of the stressor) or cooking your favourite dish. Do not try to meditate or listen to a song. Passive approaches don't work when your mind is so engrossed in 'bad thoughts.'

- **Act of Generosity**: When you are very stressed, do a 'random act of kindness' for a stranger. Buy coffee for the next person in line or send a thank you email appreciating the work of someone who never expects it from you.

- **High- intensity activity**: Engage in any intense activity that requires your body & mind to fully focus on it and nothing else – this could be a sport (my favourite is boxing since if I am boxing, I can't think of anything else, lest I get punched in the face!) or a dance. The only requirements are:

  - BOTH mind and body need to be involved – but remember, it cannot be an activity that only involves the mind, like reading, or only involves the body, like walking.

  - The level of activity has to be **intense – not mild.**

- **Laughter** is the best anti-stress medicine. Engaging in humour for 15 minutes daily is a sure-shot remedy to reduce stress levels.

- **Serenity prayer**: When you are stressed, sit down and say the following prayer:

  God, grant me the serenity to accept the things I can't change, the courage to change the things I can change and the wisdom to know the difference between the two.

> *"Most of the bad things that I imagined, never happened, but their effect on me definitely did!" (Dale Carnegie)*
>
> *"It is not stress that kills us, it is our reaction to it." (Hans Selye)*
>
> *"I stress about stress before there is anything to stress about." (Osho Rajneesh)*
>
> *"Stressed spelled backwards is Desserts – coincidence?" (Internet meme)*
>
> *"Anxiety is a part of who we are but not the full one." (Thich Nhat Hanh)*
>
> *"The only folks who don't have any stress are all found in one place and one place only – the cemetery." (Dr. Ajay Tamhane)*
>
> *"People are not disturbed by things, but by the view they take of them." (Epictetus)*
>
> *"Worrying is just a like rocking chair. It will keep you busy, but lead you nowhere." (Anonymous)*

PART C:
POST GOAL ACHIEVEMENT/ (INITIAL) FAILURE

Now, at the end of the efforts phase, you will have either succeeded or failed. This part applies in either case. If you have failed, then remember – it's all about dusting yourself off, shedding a few tears and getting back to the drawing board. The real failure is to not get back up again.

15. Enjoyment of the Process

A] Core Idea: Being obsessed with goals and milestones is a great thing. In fact, some would argue that this obsession is precisely what makes winners. While this is true, the efforts will be futile unless one also enjoys the journey. Life is too short to agonize only over the end product. To live life fully and achieve many goals, it is equally important to embrace the journey in its entirety. Otherwise, we run the risk of forgetting what made us start on the goal in the first place. As Andre Agassi sadly remarked at the end of an illustrious tennis career, "I hated tennis, but I did it since my father forced me to. And over time, I became damn good at it – yet I hated it. Probably the only good thing that came out of me playing tennis is my wife Steffi". On the other hand, Christiano Ronaldo remarked, "I would still be playing football even if no one noticed it or paid me for it. It's what I love, it's my life, and life is too big to put a price on".

B] Points to Note:

1. The first part of the enjoyment process is being aware of the process – what is happening to you as

a result of the goal that you have set? How are you feeling? What's different – in your attitude, behaviour and interactions? Are you happy with this change? Are you connected with yourself as you go on this adventure, or are you overtly focused on the endpoint and not even bothered by things around you?

2. While your goal may be getting promoted to a CXO position, the journey will entail learning different mindsets & skill sets as well as developing new relationships, networks and so on. Unless you appreciate and like these changes, you will not be able to fully accelerate your own journey.

3. On your deathbed, you will hardly say, "I am glad I became the CEO, but I messed up my family, drove away all the friends I had, developed a variety of ulcers and liver cirrhosis and by the way, I forgot to take even a short walk in the park outside my office!" You don't want to have any regrets about achieving your goals. That's why it is important to focus equally on the process as well as the results.

***

Once, an old traveller was resting under the shade of a large tree. A young boy approached and sat down next to him. "Where are you going?" asked the boy. The traveller replied, "I'm not sure where this road will lead me but I will go ahead and see."

The boy was surprised. "How can you not know where you're going? You are still making all this effort for an unknown destination?" he asked. The traveller smiled. "I don't know my destination just now, but I'm sure I'll know it when I get there. The beauty is in the journey, not the destination."

The boy still didn't understand. "But how will you know you've arrived if you don't know where you're going?" The traveller replied, "When I arrive, there will be peace and contentment in my heart. The journey is what shapes us and makes us grow."

The boy considered this. He had always focused excessively on goals and destinations, but he had never appreciated the point of being in the moment during the journey. He realized there was wisdom in the traveller's words. "I think I understand," he said. "It's not about where I'm going, but how I enjoy and view the journey."

The traveller nodded. "Our perspective shapes our reality. Choose to see each moment as an opportunity to learn and grow and appreciate the simple beauties around you. Find peace in the moment of today, not just the destination of tomorrow."

***

On a totally different note, the footballers in the following story forgot all about the moment and only focused on the tasks at hand.

Once, a bunch of drunk footballers came to a riverbank. It was late at night, and there was no boatman. However, they saw a boat with oars. Being strong and tough, they decided to row to the other bank, which was their destination.

Excited, they challenged each other, "Let's row across in less than 15 minutes."

"Yes, let's show the boatman that we don't depend on him." And off they went, shouting and screaming like the alphas. After a few hours of rowing, they were very tired, and yet they could not see the riverbank.

"We must have become slower, given our intense match earlier." They urged each other, "Let's not lose focus. We can crack this in the next thirty minutes. Come on, boys!"

A few more hours passed, and they were no closer to their goal. By now, the effects of alcohol had worn off. Suddenly, one of them looked around and said, "Oh no, we forgot to remove the anchor!"

It was only then that they realized that they had been rowing on the spot for the last several hours! No wonder they had not moved even an inch. Under the influence of alcohol, they had been so focused on the goal of reaching the other side that they had not even bothered to remove the anchor! They were not really in the moment when they embarked on their journey.

***

C] Quick Hacks:

- **Heck of it/ sake of it:** Do at least one thing that is not connected with your goal, even as you are pursuing your goal. This is for YOU and not for any other purpose. It could be a hobby, an idle pastime, anything. There should be no correlation between this and your goal – so it can't be swimming if your goal is to get fitter. It can't be meeting 1 new person every day if your goal is to be more confident in public settings. This activity has to be what you would love to do, irrespective of your goal! This is your recovery time.

- **85-year-old 'Time letter'**: Imagine that you are now 85 years old, staring at death and reflecting on the life that you have lived. Now, start writing a letter to your current self. It's like a time travel in thoughts. Assume that you have met all your goals as a backdrop to this letter. The contents of this letter will tell you what you really missed on the journey to goal achievement. Is your 85-year-old contented and composed? Are you wholeheartedly congratulating yourself for a life well-lived, or are you expressing any regrets? More often than not, these regrets will be those parts of the living process that you have missed out on, including family, relationships, hobbies, or just smelling the roses even as you walk on the streets or sipping coffee, waiting for your beloved. Don't hold back – the more explicit you are, the better you will articulate what is missing in your life. Keep reading this letter every 4-6 months to remind yourself of what's most important to the 'future YOU'.

Note: *There is definitely a counter to this principle – that of planning ahead and ALWAYS staying prepared. In one of Aesop's fables, ants chastise a grasshopper for not collecting food during the summer and suffering the consequences of famine during the cold winter. The grasshopper, who lives in the moment, admits, "I was so busy singing that I didn't have the time." Hence, it's important to find a proper balance between being in the moment and constantly planning ahead. One cannot go to either extremes of living too much in the moment and becoming unwise or ignoring TODAY for the thoughts of yesterday and tomorrow.*

> *"What is this life full of care, we have no time to stand and stare?"* (W H Davies)
>
> *"What a pity, I climbed the Himalayas but forgot to see the views on the way!"* (Anon)
>
> *"Experience of the experience is a profound experience."* (Sadguru Jaggi Vasudev)
>
> *"Process satisfaction is more important than end goal satisfaction."* (Dr. Ajay Tamhane)

16. Lose – But Don't Lose the Lesson & Never Give Up!

A⟩ **Core idea:** The goal that you set is never the 'final one' – this holds true whether you achieve it at first go or not. The question is, when you failed, did you learn the lesson? Did you incorporate the learnings? Did you understand why you failed and what you would do differently the next time?

According to one version of history, the Afghan warlord Muhammad Ghori failed to win against the Rajput King Prithviraj Chauhan twenty times. Did he give up? Never. Instead, he kept modifying his techniques and strategies until he finally won decisively on his 21st attack. J.K. Rowling, the famous author of the Harry Potter series, was rejected by twelve publishers for the first book in the series, but she also never gave up.

In 1985, Steve Jobs was fired from the company he had created. This gave him the chance to reassess and start from scratch with new projects, like NeXT and Pixar. Eventually, he re-entered Apple and became the CEO, showing that passion can be stronger than failure. He also used technologies he developed at Pixar to develop a lot of the next-generation stuff at Apple.

Walt Disney was told that he wasn't creative enough. His business, Laugh-O-Gram, went bankrupt. He essentially hit rock bottom and almost contemplated suicide until he found success with Mickey Mouse in Steamboat Willie. His next success was with Snow

White and the Seven Dwarfs, which went on to win eight Oscars.

Lastly, the legend goes that the great scientist Thomas Alva Edison tried more than 950+ times to invent the light bulb. Every time he failed, he would mutter something, go home and come back the next day with greater enthusiasm. His assistants lost patience with his behaviour. "Sir, how is it that you continue to be so patient despite so many failures?" They demanded, "What do you say to yourself after each time?" Smiling, Edison said, "Each time we fail, I say to myself, Excellent. Now I know one more way NOT to make the bulb glow. Let's learn the lessons and move on!" His assistants were speechless. Many years later, there was a fire in Edison's lab that destroyed many of his important papers – of which there were no copies or duplicates. As everyone tried frantically to salvage what they could, Edison smiled to himself and drank coffee. Again, his harassed assistants asked, "Sir, we have had a tragedy, and yet you continue to smile! How is this possible?"

"Many of my mistakes have gone up in flames," Edison said happily, "Now, I can start afresh!"

Forget celebrities – each one of us understands this concept at a genetic level, but we just fail to implement it in real life. The human DNA has evolved through a series of failures and subsequent adaptations, which has made us the most dominant species on the planet. This couldn't have happened if we had not failed umpteen times. Our entire existence is essentially a tribute to the human spirit of failing, learning, adapting and rising up stronger than ever.

B] Points to Note:

1. When one fails, it is important to step back and take stock. What went wrong? Could you have prepared for it? Was it a failure of strategy, tactics, mindset or was it just plain bad luck? How does one ensure that this does not get repeated again?

2. *Lose the battle, win the war*, but you will need to learn the right lessons from the loss. Acceptance of the loss is the first step towards improving the chances of victory the next time.

3. Failure is not the end of the road but a 'pause time' to reflect – the insights learnt from personal failure are invaluable if only we are humble enough to learn from them.

4. While one side of failure is disappointment, disillusionment and frustration, the other side of failure is growth, change and progress. Can we look at both these sides in a balanced manner? It is very natural to feel sad, upset, and angry at failure, but can we overcome it by viewing each failure as a learning opportunity?

C] Quick Hacks:

o **Post-mortem analysis**: This involves a detailed analysis of the loss by considering the reasons at length. More importantly, the assessment is not just of the reasons but also potential mitigations that could/should have been done and a mention of what needs to be done next time. If done correctly, it can ensure that the failure is not in vain. The biggest risk is that if not done well, this may become a blame game, creating its own set of troubles.

- **Socratic inputs** (also explained earlier in a different context): This involves talking with 5 key well-wishers/ stakeholders who are aware of your situation and asking them why they thought you failed and what they would suggest you do next time. It was said that Socrates used to apply this method when he was faced with complex problems and dilemmas, especially ones where he felt that his own view was likely to be biased. Getting multiple perspectives reduces this risk. Our biases often blind us to the real reasons behind failure. Some of the most common biases contributing to our inability to analyse failure include:

    - Confirmation bias: We go out looking for something that we have always held true without checking for the converse (e.g., we believe that we lost because someone, say the umpire, was partial to our opponent)

    - Hindsight bias: Everything is clear in hindsight. The issue is why we were not able to discover this before the task was undertaken.

    - Superman bias: One believes that even when 100 others have failed at a task, one will succeed because he/she is 'special.'

    - Halo effect: Just because one is good at something makes one believe that he/she is good at everything.

> *"Success is not final; failure is not fatal – it is the courage to continue that counts." (Churchill)*
>
> *"It's not whether you get knocked down – it's whether you get back up after the knock." (Lombardi)*
>
> *"Failure is not the OPPOSITE of success. It is an integral PART of success."*
>
> *"Failure is not fatal, but failure to change might be." (John Wooden)*
>
> *"Only those who learn to fail greatly can ever achieve greatly." (Robert F. Kennedy)*
>
> *"The Phoenix must burn first to emerge." (Janet Fitch)*
>
> *"If you want to increase your success, double your failure rate." (Thomas J. Watson)*

17. Happiness – The Final Frontier

A] Core Idea: Unless we are happy, at least to a certain extent, we are unlikely to perform to our fullest potential. Winners are essentially happy people. Unfortunately, there is no 'scale of happiness' though several have tried (incl. the country of Bhutan, which came up with the concept of the Gross Happiness Index) to build one.

Like all things, there is a balance required here – if we are 'too happy and contented', there is no fire in the belly or hunger to perform. Similarly, if we are extremely unhappy, without any hope or positive energy, we are unlikely to be able to focus on the goals at hand.

Finally, another way to look at this is that at the end of all the achievements and success, if we are not happy, what was the point of the struggle, the trials and the tribulations? Was it all for nothing? Happiness is what we are aspiring for at the end of the day. Without it, nothing matters.

***

Recipe for Happiness: Making Tea

Boil your Ego,

Evaporate your Worries/ Fears,

Dilute your Sorrows,

Filter your Mistakes, and

what you get is the Taste of Happiness.

***

B] Points to Note:

1. Happiness is a feeling – though it is "all in the mind", we can definitely see the visible symptoms of someone who is happy – a smile on the face, contentment in the eyes, a zing in the step, an ability to enjoy life, talk & connect well with others.

2. Interestingly, happiness has little to do in absolute terms with factors like wealth, comfort, looks, and relationships. Of course, a certain minimum amount of wealth/financial stability is needed for happiness, but beyond that number (estimated at between USD 45-80,000, depending on the country), there is no correlation. Similarly, one can find happy people amongst terminally ill cancer patients, as well as depressed millionaires and suicidal rockstars who haven't been happy for years.

3. Philosophers and spiritual proponents often classify happiness into 2 categories – inner happiness (contentment, the right mindset, lack of feelings of inadequateness, insecurity, greed, etc.) and outer happiness (success, fame, wealth)

4. Happiness as a concept has several 'cousins,' including success, well-being, contentment, satisfaction etc. While I won't delve deeper into each of these and the differences between them and happiness, the important point is that while one may not always be able to spot a 'happy person', it is easier to spot an unhappy person!

***

A woodcutter went into the forest in search of ordinary wood. At the entrance, he saw a monk meditating in silence.

As he was passing the monk, the woodcutter requested the monk to tell him where he could find some trees to cut since that was his primary source of livelihood.

The monk replied, "Just a few metres ahead, you will find teakwood."

The woodcutter followed his suggestion and found the teakwood exactly as the monk had promised. Satisfied with his day's work, he thought to himself later, "I went in search of ordinary wood and got teakwood! Wow, what luck!"

The next day, he thanked the monk and asked him, "Where can I find more teakwood?"

The monk replied, "If you go slightly deeper inside the forest, you will find sandalwood."

And just like that, the woodcutter found the sandalwood.

He returned home, thrilled.

The next day as soon as he asked, the monk said, "If you go deeper still, you will find lots of silver and gold."

The woodcutter's excitement knew no bounds and he took home heaps of silver and gold. He was now a rich man, thanks to the monk.

The next day, when he asked about more silver and gold, the monk said, "If you go even deeper, you will find precious stones - emeralds, rubies, sapphires and diamonds."

The woodcutter was dazed and also a bit surprised.

He asked the monk, "If you know where all these treasures are available in the forest, why are you not going for them? Why are you sitting here?"

The monk simply smiled and continued his meditation.

It was then that the woodcutter realized that the monk had his own priceless treasure: inner happiness!

Awestruck and inspired, the woodcutter joined the monk in solitude – and soon, he too found the happiness within.

***

C] **Quick Hacks**:

o **A chemist's approach to happiness**: There are 4 'happiness chemicals' & we can increase our happiness by increasing the levels of each of these chemicals in our brains:

- Oxytocin *(aka love hormone)* is generated through relationships, family time, connections, romantic attraction, cuddling babies, playing with pets, and sex.

- Serotonin *(aka mood stabilizer) is* generated through exposure to the sun, proper food, good digestion, meditation, and nature walks.

- Dopamine *(aka reward chemical)* is generated through momentary arousals (e.g., WhatsApp messages, emails) as well as task completion, achievement of goals, and celebrating milestones.

- Endorphins (*aka pain reducer*) are generated through physical exercise ("runner's high" or the "lifter's paradise"), laughter, and watching a scary movie.

o **A philosopher's approach to happiness**

- Happiness Index = (Number of desires met)/(Number of desires generated)

- Hence, we either try to meet as many of our desires (focus on the numerator) as possible OR reduce the number of desires generated in the first place (focus on the denominator). Most of us work only on the numerator, i.e., meeting desires and ignore the denominator, i.e., reducing the number of desires generated in the first place.

o **'Small guide' approach to happiness**: Do small acts of kindness every day + learn to savour the small things in life (e.g., a sunset, a nice conversation, a beautiful song, a caring touch, a cup of freshly brewed coffee). Small things go a long way on the road to happiness.

o **CFD-GFD-JFD approach to happiness**:

- Complaint Free Day – 1 day in the month is to be explicitly tagged as a complaint-free one, where one does not crib, criticize, play the victim card, or be negative.

- Gratitude-Filled Day – 1 day in the month be explicitly tagged where we express gratitude and appreciation for all the things we take for granted (our health, our partners, our support system, nature)

- Joy-Filled Day – if you are able to do CFD and GFD above, then you are entitled to a JFD, a day in which you indulge yourself with 3 of your personal favourites (e.g., 1 movie + 1 ice cream and 1 massage). This day has to be earned based on the earlier two.

- Once you have done these 3 days every month for about 3-4 months, you can move on to doing them every week – believe me, it is challenging but well worth it from a happiness standpoint.

> "Happiness is a choice – life will happen irrespective of whether you choose to be happy or not." (Anonymous)
>
> "Happiness *is like a butterfly which, when pursued, is always beyond our grasp, but, if you sit down quietly, may alight upon you.*" (Nathaniel Hawthorne)
>
> "Remember this, that very little is needed to make a happy life." (Marcus Aurelius)

***

As we close:

Let me end with the story of the million dollar horse.

A long time ago, in the markets of Baghdad, came a horse-seller with several horses. His collection attracted the attention of several buyers, including that of the Prince, who happened to be strolling in the market at that very moment.

The Prince began enquiring about the prices of various steeds, and the seller gave him the required information.

Most of the horses ranged between 10,000 darics and 50,000 darics. The Prince contemplated buying a few for his royal stable. Just as he was about to close the deal, he saw a black stallion standing far away from the others. The stallion was tall, strong, and robust.

How much is that horse for?" enquired the Prince.

"Oh, that one. It is a very rare horse", said the merchant. "Normally, I would not even offer it for sale, given its value".

"Oh, come on. Don't you know who I am? Name the price, and I will pay it", replied the Prince.

"Ok, your Highness. If you insist, I bought this horse from a sorcerer in the mountains of Zagros for 1 million darics, and I am willing to sell it at the same price to your Highness", said the merchant.

"One million darics? Are you out of your mind? What does this horse do that it commands such an exorbitant price? Can it fly in the sky, or does it have magical powers?" enquired the Prince.

"It does neither of the two activities, your Highness", replied the merchant politely. "However, it can do lots of other things".

"Like?" asked the Prince.

"Oh, the horse can recite the Koran flawlessly. He can also play chess well. He can also understand if there is a storm coming and warn its rider accordingly. He can do many more miracles like this if he wants to", replied the merchant sheepishly.

"I can't believe it. You are bluffing", said the Prince.

"No, my Lord. Everything that I say is 100 per cent true. The horse can do all of what I said and more, if he wants to", said the merchant.

"OK, I will buy the horse and test if everything that you claim is true. If not, you have had it. I will not spare your life", said the Prince.

"Of course, your Highness. Why would I lie to you? You can take the horse home and assess its prowess yourself", said the merchant.

The Prince paid the million darics and took the horse to the royal palace. Later in the day, he asked the horse to recite the Koran. The horse only made a few sounds and stood in its place. Then, the Prince laid out a game of chess before the horse and played a move, waiting for the horse to respond. The horse did not do anything. Frustrated, the Prince asked his servant to whip the horse. No sooner was the horse whipped than he kicked the chessboard, scattering all the pieces. The Prince was getting extremely angry at the moment. As a last resort, he asked the horse to tell his future. The horse merely neighed and looked blankly at the ground.

Now, the Prince lost his cool totally. "Guards, arrest the merchant who sold me this horse and bring him to me immediately. I will teach that scoundrel a lesson".

The guards ran to the market to find the merchant. They were directed to a nearby lodge where the merchant was supposedly staying for the night. The guards went to the lodge and enquired about the merchant's room.

The lodge keeper sheepishly said, "His room was on the first floor. The last one on the right. However, he just left a few hours back, so no point in going there".

The guards were now worried. They were scared to return to the palace empty-handed. Just as they were discussing the matter amongst themselves, the lodge-keeper said, "Sirs, the honourable gentleman left something for the Prince. He told me that just in case the Prince or his men came looking, I was to hand this scroll over to you".

Relieved, the guards snatched the scroll and returned to the palace.

"Your Highness, the merchant was nowhere to be found. However, he has left this scroll for you", replied the chief.

Furiously, the Prince opened the scroll. It read as follows:

Dear Prince, you may be upset that the horse has not done any of the activities that I told you about. Hence, you may feel like accusing me of cheating. Trust me, your Highness. I have not cheated you at all. The truth is that the horse can absolutely recite the scriptures, play chess, foretell the future, and many more things. However, as I had clearly mentioned, he does so ONLY when he wants to do it. No one and nothing can force him to do anything. So, my humble request is that you hope and pray that the horse feels like doing the things you or anyone else wants him to. Moreover, don't bother trying to find me for I have long left the country and sailed across the seas".

The Prince sat down with a heavy sigh.

No power in the universe can really force you to act on your goals, dreams, and desires – ONLY YOU CAN. The question is, WILL YOU?

END *(Effort Never Dies)*

Acknowledgements
(and some Apologies)

I would like to acknowledge our families for being the pillars of support they have been as we have embarked on this and other journeys that took us away from spending precious time with them.

Firstly, loads of kisses and hugs to Asya and Ehaan Tamhane, who bore the absence of their father and grandfather, or more accurately, the presence of the two male members, locked up in the study, trying to complete the book. This led to us not being able to join some of the critical school functions and family moments. So sorry, kiddos.

Huge gratitude to my mother, Dr. Jayashree Tamhane, who gave up her flourishing medical career to take care of our household and focus on my upbringing. She gave up her goals so that I could achieve mine.

A very special thanks to my wife, Deepti, for being so gracious and allowing me to take time out for the book despite her hectic schedule as a start-up founder and homemaker. Hats off to her multi-tasking! She also motivated me to NOT give up on the dream of writing a book in 24 hours and ensured that she chipped away at every excuse of mine. Again, a small note of apology to Deepti also since the process of finishing this book did take me away from several of the household chores that were on my plate, but I ducked them citing book completion as a convenient excuse.

I would also like to thank Mridula Arvind for helping complement the various concepts with her extensive experiences as a practising psychologist and counsellor. Mridula and her husband, Arvind, help thousands of aspirants achieve their goals through multiple initiatives like seminars, personal counselling and mind training.

I am grateful to my editor, Narayani Basu, for her invaluable assistance in proofreading and editing the manuscript in a timely manner and enabling me to convert a rough draft into a readable book. I am also thankful to Blue Rose Publishers for giving me the platform to publish the book.

Lastly, to all the goal seekers and achievers out there – this book is BY you and FOR you. Hope you enjoy and benefit from reading it as much as I enjoyed writing it. A big thanks and best wishes to you – crack it big!

As my hero, Edmund Hillary, said, *"It is not the mountain that we conquer but ourselves in the process"* - so also, through this book, we have overcome our fears of finally taking up the 24-hour challenge and putting on paper something we have believed in for the longest time – it is possible!

www.ingramcontent.com/pod-product-compliance
Lightning Source LLC
LaVergne TN
LVHW041847070526
838199LV00045BA/1487